The

Bitcoin

Manifesto

The

Bitcoin

Manifesto

ALLAN STEVO

Editorial Assistant & Layout: Jarrett Smith,
Ivana Hirjáková

Cover Design: Zizi Iryaspraha Subiyarta

Crafting52

Chicago • Bratislava • New York

ISBN-13: 978-1539595137

ISBN-10: 1539595137

CONTENTS

The

Bitcoin

Manifesto

The False Prophets Of Bitcoin

Talk of Bitcoin is full of lies. *The Wall Street Journal* tells lies. Its staunchest advocates tell lies. Few seem to grasp the potential of Bitcoin, which is fine; it simply indicates shortsightedness. Even more are too lazy, intellectually, to seek the truth. That's a less comfortable position to observe. Such people speak and repeat platitudes for and against Bitcoin, and we are left with fast-talkers generating heat in futile discussions, rather than shedding light. At their very core they demonstrate one reason why Bitcoin is so important – it removes a need for trust. It removes the need to trust a third party. Many who speak the word "Bitcoin" are not trustworthy, whether for or against.

In 2008, many voters felt trust for Barack Obama. None of them knew Barack Obama personally, so to trust him was naive. Few men deserve trust. Whorishly, we give that sacred asset cheaply. As if we could not live another minute without giving a person our trust, we do away with the very natural emotions of skepticism, suspicion, and self-protection. Few deserve that trust and certainly no man deserves unearned trust.

And if no man deserves unearned trust, dare I suggest that a company, organization, or financial institution deserves unearned trust? Most certainly not. After all, they are only a collection of men and women who have not earned trust. Yet that is exactly what takes place virtually each time we engage in interaction as simple as online commerce or deal with nearly any entity in the financial services industry.

Bring back the run on the bank – they deserve no trust. FDIC insurance is a scam, since it can't really deliver on what it promises. It is unable to handle systemic shock, only individual banks falling apart. Public trust is placed in a dollar undeserving of trust. What backs it? Gold in Fort Knox we've never seen? A military might we cannot trust run by a large, unfamiliar Department of Defense? Central bankers having closed-door meetings, secretively lending $16 trillion in newly created money to foreign banks? Decisions in each of these areas are made by political leaders who we've never met for more than a minute – and that's if you're lucky. The dollar is a method of wealth transmission undeserving of trust.

Yet we do trust it and those several institutions mentioned. We almost have no choice but to deal with them. We could operate in a barter economy for our existence. We could stay up at night worrying whether this will be one of those moments where a financial institution is about to be proven untrustworthy. We could simply forget about the shortcomings of the system since there's no credible alternative. None of these options are attractive.

That's where Bitcoin comes in. Sort of a money 2.0, the way the Internet is a library 2.0. Both statements are a gross under-exaggeration of the true potential of the technology underpinning those systems. The Internet is much more than a library and Bitcoin is much more than money. The people quickest to realize this will also be the ones to understand the inevitability that a better financial system will spring from the Bitcoin protocol. Those who act on that realization will have a very bright future ahead for themselves.

Dominate With Great Energy Today

Drop everything you are doing and move into the Bitcoin space. Put down your plow and follow. Put down your nets. The moneychangers' tables are about to be overturned. The men at the gates are about to lose their walls. A revolution is taking place.

It's not the futile protests of free-speech zones. It's not a sit-in at a government building. It's the kind of revolution that strikes men deep. It's the kind of revolution that easily motivates others to join in by appealing to self-interest and desire. Walmart did not become great because of marches on Neiman Marcus. Nor will the Federal Reserve Bank fall from protest marches. One hundred years of complaining about the Fed have proven futile. Great change happens because the new replaces the old by better appealing to the wants of society.

Those who come today to lead that revolution in finance, in more secure online interaction, in microbanking, in contracts, signatures, escrow, and distributed autonomous corporations, in a host of areas affected by this new protocol will have umpteen times greater odds of being the billionaires and trillionaires of tomorrow.

Move now. Dominate now. Whatever you think your role is, play it now. Stop spending time and money frivolously. Do everything you can to form an area of specialization for yourself in the Bitcoin space, as much as possible, as quickly as possible. He who wakes every morning asking, "How can I make Bitcoin faster, stronger, more flexible, and in any other way better?" will be among those who change the world.

Bitcoin is Not A Charity

Some Bitcoin events feel like Woodstock. They feel like a campaign of idealistic youth. They feel ideological. Make no mistake about it: Bitcoin is no charity. Bitcoin is about money. Some in Bitcoin forget that. By putting your passions to work, in a burgeoning industry, you can generate the resources needed to last and prosper in that industry. Many who fail to realize this will soon be gone, left bitter that their hard work never paid off. Most of what they did, though, was talk and cheerlead, so there's little for anyone to be upset about.

Entrepreneurs act. They streamline ineffi-ciencies in economies, delivering aid, benefit, and value to paying consumers, making themselves a tremendous amount of money in the process. Are you a cheerleader or an entrepreneur? Are you a talker or a doer?

Like many people, you're probably the latter –
so far.

In most areas of life, that's a fine position to
be in. Talkers are rewarded. In the fast-moving
Bitcoin space, it's a different story. In fact, if
you don't shift away from talking and towards
doing, you will forever be given the punish-
ment of watching the world pass you by as
you hear a Johnny-come-lately speaking on
the news about a great idea *you* once had –
and all because he was a more aggressive
entrepreneur than you and not a squawking
cheerleader. The more successful the idea, the
more you will be reminded of what could have
been. The early adopters are rewarded if they
monetize. They are rewarded if they appeal to
a consumer and add value. The early adopters
cum entrepreneurs are the winners. The others
will still be cheerleading fifty years from now –

poor, or of mediocre wealth, telling their grandkids about how they were "right there." Loving grandkids will smile admiringly, as it won't be until they reach a certain age that they will come to understand that Grandpa was there in the right place at the right moment in history, but that he was a cheerleader instead of an entrepreneur.

The world needs cheerleaders. It takes such little ability to be a cheerleader that the world quite understandably forgets the cheerleader and focuses on those who achieve great things. Those who come early to an industry and make great things happen will hold coveted positions. Being but a cheerleader in a fast-paced environment leaves one in a vulnerable state of weakness.

Enter The Shark

Sharks smell weakness. They smell blood. They feel the flopping around of a slowly dying creature. They take advantage of situations and dominate. Seasoned commodities traders, investment bankers, and entrepreneurs have entered the exciting Bitcoin space and are prepared to dominate. They've been through a few failures in their time and maybe a success or two. They know the difference between the two and know how to win at this game of startups and market making.

Sharks have an advantage over some. Having specific knowledge of Bitcoin and knowing how to apply that knowledge for the benefit of a consumer in exchange for profit allows you to stand out and to have an advantageous position of your own. If you are reading this, you likely already understand a niche in Bitcoin a little bit better than your average-Joe investment banker. No matter how big a shark that average-Joe investment banker is, you, by virtue of your chance position in life, might "get" Bitcoin a little better.

Now is your chance. Identify a problem and move to solve it. The Bitcoin space will not remain untouched forever. If you do not take this chance to give yourself a head start, when a shark catches you, you'll one day regret the time you squandered. It's time you could have spent working on that head start in those days when few understood Bitcoin. Ready or not, the sharks are coming. The shark might overtake you today or the shark might overtake you tomorrow. That is a risk. With luck and hard, quick work you'll be someone that never happens to.

No Barrier To Entry

It doesn't have to be like that. There's very little barrier to entry in Bitcoin. Anyone can own Bitcoin ten minutes from now. Anyone can learn to code with just days of effort. Anyone can understand Bitcoin in minutes. Sitting smugly, looking out at the world because of your advanced knowledge may be comfortable, but there should be no pride in doing so. You could, right now, be implementing your Bitcoin-related ideas instead of reading. I encourage you to do exactly that. Avert your eyes and come back to read this after you've made your first billion.

You see, that billion will be proof of something: it will be proof of value. Our economy tends to reward those who provide value to consumers. Value is a synonym for helping. Help is not often a word we equate with profit.

Help is exactly what that is though – helping consumers solve a problem, sometimes a problem they didn't even realize they had.

Help is no less valuable when done for profit or any other form of self-interest. In fact, I've long ago realized – and maybe you have too – that people tend to help a little more diligently when there is money on the line. A sense of duty and responsibility tends to come out more diligently when money is involved. When profit is involved, it suddenly becomes an even bigger priority to help. Whereas at other times, help might be an occasional hassle or even just an endeavor you sometimes put half a heart into.

But there's more to doing well than just profit. There's passion too. It's a lucky man who makes his living developing his passions.

Making money in Bitcoin feels pretty good. The good you know you personally have brought into the world, the value you have created for others, the help you have given so many consumers, and the inspiration you have provided to others through your competitive spirit – that is what that first billion represents. "The end is nothing; the road is all" wrote French historian Jules Michelet nearly two centuries ago.

The opportunity for following your passion and commanding profit stands right in front of your face, waiting for you to take your reward. It's your reward in exchange for dominating a niche in the Bitcoin space and delivering superior value to consumers. Of course, when all goes well, you do more than simply make a living while using your passions to provide value to consumers. You get very rich, and deservedly so.

In the grand scheme of things, the money means relatively little. What you did to get that money means much. Money is a good motivator, a good simple goal, especially when it motivates people to change the world by helping their fellow man through the often effective equation of an entrepreneur getting paid to develop a product that will create utility for a consumer.

Unlike 99.9998 percent of people in the US, you have an inside tip, a glimpse into the future potential of a growing industry that most people have never even heard of. Few understand that industry.

So much the better that few people currently understand Bitcoin. Great wealth, generational wealth, Rockefeller wealth, Kennedy influence were all built in markets few understood. They defied what the moderates found decent. They also made so much money unabashedly that they eventually came to dictate what was decent. They did so by eventually being powerful enough to write the laws. In the absence of more legitimate forms of moral authority, the laws came to dictate what would be considered decent to many. In doing so, future generations had little ability to gauge that indecency.

The behaviors that made families like the Kennedys or Rockefellers rich and influential was seen by some as indecent. Looking back on it later, such denunciations last for what would seem like only a moment in time. How ashamed some must feel coming from great fortunes made "indecently." Such pioneers become the changemakers who move society. The shame disappears, society forgets, and the great fortunes remain. A handful know what patriarchs of families like these know. These are the ones who beat out their competitors in fringe and developing industries.

You today are in a place like that. Embrace the potential of that setting in which you find yourself. You are a Kennedy, you are a Rockefeller. Whatever strange-sounding last name you possess will be tomorrow's household name.

Smashed By Liars, Praised By Liars

To dominate a terrain, you need a true map and a compass that you've used to orient yourself. Reality always presents us with challenges that need overcoming. These challenges require of us a realistic assessment of the situation along with a realistic assessment of our own skills and resources. The skills required to be dominant in the Bitcoin space are minimal, largely because it is such new territory.

The resources needed are all around us in this easy-money economy at a time in history where programming skills abound and powerful programs can be built even on simple laptops. What is left then to overcome any challenging terrain is simply an honest assessment of that terrain. Honest assessments of the Bitcoin space are in short supply.

Cheerleaders with an axe to grind either for or against Bitcoin offer the most vocal assessments and correspondingly create distortions that are not based on fact. Addressing some of those distortions and their perpetuators is important in identifying our true location in the midst of our terrain.

Cheerleading

During an American political campaign I once helped with, morning commutes were heavy and train stations made for excellent campaigning. Our canvassers could talk to voters for more than the usual ten or fifteen seconds. Future constituents had time and interest in talking while waiting for a train. They were affluent, well-educated, well-connected voters.

These conversations proved a disheartening trend. Watching the talking points of the presidential campaigns – Obama/Biden, McCain/Palin and their surrogates in the media Friday, Saturday, and Sunday was an excellent predictor of what would be discussed Monday at the train station.

A topic that voters had never cared about – usually something insignificant – would be brought up over the weekend in the media only to have the talking points of the campaigns parroted Monday at the train station. When you hear thirty people at a train station tell you the exact same thing hours apart from each other, and saying it as passionately and sincerely as if it were his or her own original idea, you start to take note.

Lots of cheerleading takes place in American society. Even well-educated affluent people do little more than cheerlead and parrot on a variety of topics, and do so with such arrogance. They also denigrate new ideas on demand as if they shared a central brain in a network somewhere.

This groupthink is just as damaging when it is positive as when it is negative.

The community of people around Bitcoin risk sounding a lot like those voters at the train station. Some abide by the rule, "You may not say an unkind word about Bitcoin." They often kick it up a notch by adding something along the lines of, "You must use only superlatives, and they must be positive." They lie to themselves and others and deserve the lack of credibility earned by liars. You might call it sales, spin, or talking points. I come from a place where we eschew those politician-friendly euphemisms. We just call it lying.

No thinking person should be a cheerleader either for or against Bitcoin. There's no need for it. The facts are already so good that the lies and the fallacious sales pitch are ridiculous. Why lie when the truth is already so good?

Bitcoin itself can be better than lying politicians. That's part of what makes Bitcoin so good. It provides a technology that seeks to go beyond the need for trust.

Bitcoin Isn't A Great Investment

To the chagrin of my colleagues in the Bitcoin industry, I don't buy into the hype. I'm not a true believer. Bitcoin – the currency – is not that new and interesting of an investment.

I'm a seasoned investor. I have been reading stock quotes and annual reports since childhood. I recognize Bitcoin to be a poor investment for me. Below are a few reasons.

1. I have no idea what moves the Bitcoin market – maybe it's purely speculative behavior from people with no rational concept of how to price the product.
2. The value of the technology is enormous; I'm not certain that correlates to the value of Bitcoin as a currency.
3. The price is far beyond what I see as the fundamentals of the currency.

4. The price of Bitcoin, the currency, naturally fluctuates wildly as price discovery takes place in a relatively small market.
5. I have little certainty that the price (at any level) will remain there.
6. It is all risk and questionable reward.
7. Its market is incredibly small and therefore subject to manipulation.

Black-box algos are perfect for this market. I don't like trading those markets, especially not today when there is so much money everywhere that virtually anyone can make a killing, even in relatively safe investments. The risk of being long Bitcoin in that environment doesn't make sense.

Bitcoin is a terrible investment for me and a terrible investment for everyone I know. It may shoot to $100,000 / Bitcoin tomorrow. That won't change anything that I am saying here and will even further prove that I don't understand its movements, further proving it a bad investment for me. It will remain just as unpredictable an investment. Bitcoin will go to zero, or to many zeroes. No one is quite sure which of those extremes may take place, but it seems likely that it will find itself at one extreme or the other. That's not investing; that's gambling – so for the time being, I will only buy and trade Bitcoin using the small percentage of my portfolio that I reserve for gambling.

Some of the adults I know putting their money in Bitcoin are going through experiences I went through in my teens, such as dealing with gambler's fallacy or being schooled because they lack a basic understanding of technical analysis. Learning a new skill is great. Acting like you are a veteran when you aren't isn't that impressive and can appear transparent.

The Bitcoin community abounds with what I consider to be some of the most amateur stories of people not understanding what they have right in front of them:

- Terrible market timing, and using no technique for mitigating that terrible market timing.
- Not securing their investments.
- Approaching investing with no investment strategy.
- Stories of people throwing away Bitcoin.
- Stories of people misplacing Bitcoin wallets, but recalling how many Bitcoin they had.
- Losing a password, forgetting a password, or simply setting a password so

haphazardly that the wallet owner can't ever duplicate the password in order to log in to a wallet a second time.

These stories are evidence that Bitcoin is not even taken that seriously by some of its staunchest advocates. They don't take it seriously enough to learn to protect their Bitcoin-based wealth or even to learn basic trading strategies to treat the investment wisely. Some of its staunchest advocates treat it like monopoly money, which consequently is a self-fulfilling prophesy that Bitcoin tends to follow.

Those new to Bitcoin can easily sense this lack of seriousness, this lack of investment, this experimental attitude toward Bitcoin. For many seasoned investors, investing is not a joke, but a serious way to magnify the effectiveness of profitable work and to liberate oneself from reliance on money. Those involved in a Bitcoin community that lacks seriousness should not be surprised when that community fails to attract the serious investor. A community like that perpetuates the concept that Bitcoin is a joke. If you believe Bitcoin is nothing but a joke, then it's good to perpetuate that.

Obsessing Over The Price Of Bitcoin Is A Distraction

There is more to Bitcoin than the currency – which, again, is a poor currency. It can be fun to watch the news during an election, because it is so often reported as a horse race. This is especially fun when you have a dog in the fight. It can be fun to be invested in the stock market with its daily fluctuations egged on by usually unimportant news, especially when you have some skin in the game.

Bitcoin, the currency, turns into a horse race. Are you making a good bet? Did you win? Did you come out ahead for the day? Horse races are fun. The Bitcoin horse race is a distraction from the work that needs to be done around Bitcoin to improve the fundamentals of the currency (namely its usefulness as a currency) and to make it more than just another horserace created by a temporary bubble of weak-handed investors who seem to have too much discretionary cash on hand. The energy of the Bitcoin horse race is fun. Fun has its place. Fun can make a person smile. Smiling is good. Seeing an even more useful Bitcoin currency functioning in the world would make me smile in a different way. It wouldn't just be fun; it would be fulfilling.

The World's Most Important Digital Currency

Recently, on a visit to the Federal Reserve Bank, a US Congressman commented that he disagreed with the country's loose money policy, saying, "The Fed is printing too much money." The Federal Reserve Bank official he was speaking to corrected him, saying, "Oh, no, Congressman, we couldn't possibly *print* all the money we're *creating*."

The response was semantic. These two did not speak the same language. Money printing is a euphemism used commonly by harder money proponents in US politics to refer to "money creation."

Of course, when policies like Quantitative Easing – a longtime Fed policy even before that name existed – are put into place, extra digits are just typed into a computer and wired to a bank account before being wired to many other bank accounts and distributed throughout the economy. For years the US dollar has been the world's largest digital currency. At this stage in its existence, we should be truthful in recognizing that *Bitcoin doesn't even come close to competing with the world's largest and most important digital currency – the US dollar.*

A Solid Line

So many people talk about the great ideas they have for Bitcoin. In general, in every industry, the people who implement great ideas aren't spending much time talking about them. They are spending their time acting on those ideas. They rely on others to talk about their ideas for them. Until the idea has turned a profit, changed the world, or in some way monetized itself, the doers tend to focus and to do. A solid line exists between the talkers and the doers.

Bitcoin is a new and fascinating technology that may revolutionize the world. This leads some to confuse this fact with Bitcoin's investment potential. Bitcoin is not a new style of investment vehicle. It moves up and down erratically and can be invested in in tiny denominations with little underlying value. That sounds a lot like a penny stock.

There are many companies that have done well in turning a profit and have done well for society that haven't always made good investments.

Zenith, founded in 1918, was long respected as America's number two television manufacturer behind RCA. It had a longstanding reputation for building products of impressive quality. Additionally, it was an innovator frequently developing new products and getting them to market first; for example, it was the first company to offer subscription television service, the first portable radio, the first mass-produced AC radio, first push-button tuning radio, first wireless remote, one of the first FM stations in the US, one of the first HDTVs in North America. Zenith was a longtime dog of a stock, ripe for hostile takeover. In 1990, LG bought five percent of the company and in 1995 upped its ownership to a majority stake. The remainder of the company was purchased by LG in 1999 and Zenith filed for Chapter 11 bankruptcy.

Qualcomm is a champion innovator that even creates technologies long before consumers have any practical use for those technologies. The miniscule size and incredible functionality of so many of today's electronic products are a direct result of Qualcomm's innovation. Had you purchased Qualcomm on the open on March 29, 2000 for $158.25, taking into account the two-for-one split that occurred on July 23, 2004, you would have lost 5.2 percent, with it trading at $75 at the time this book went to press. Over those 5,046 days that you held on to that stock, that would have been an annualized loss of 0.4 percent even before inflation.

The NASDAQ traded at 5,408.60, before closing at 5,048.62 on March 10, 2000. It closed at 4,103.88 when this book went to press. Had you held on to the index for those 5,075 days, you would have lost twenty-four percent of your investment before inflation, which comes to a two percent annualized loss.

Oracle, the company that has created one of the greatest fortunes in the world, a fortune belonging to Larry Ellison, has thrived as a company without going anywhere near its April 7, 2000 close of $87.12. October 13, 2000 it split two for one, which, when sold today at $38.08, 5,038 days after purchase, would bring you an annualized loss of one percent – again not taking into account the depreciated value of the dollar due to inflation.

Burning through venture capital without ever having reached a profit was the story of so many failed Internet startups at the turn of the century. Subtract the presence of venture capital and you have the story of the overwhelming majority of small businesses. Turning a profit is an important function of a for-profit company, as the name would suggest. Entrepreneurs tend to lose focus of that fact and by the time the funding has dried up, a great product loses the support of potential investors because the management has not shown the discipline to turn a profit. Those with financial discipline to last through the ups and downs in the market and in funding tend to last – and, ultimately, lasting is a key ingredient in dominating.

Amazon.com paints a different picture and has far surpassed its old high, trading $407.05 at the time this book went to print. If purchased on the close on March 27, 2000 and held for those 5,047 days, the stock would have earned you 13.2 percent annualized.

Bubbles come into play when you talk about Bitcoin and bad investments. Both are worth reading about extensively if investing in Bitcoin is a key focus of your efforts.

Some in the Bitcoin community will say that Bitcoin is a different type of investment animal. I disagree. New takes on bad investments have long existed. Bitcoin, the currency, is just another example of that.

Bitcoin Is A Bad Currency

1. Price isn't stable.

2. Not widely adopted.

3. May never be widely adopted.

4. Poor store of value.

5. Flawed as a medium of exchange, unless the transaction is very quick.

6. Lots of friction in and out.

7. Hard to spend.

8. Risks being declared illegal as a currency.

Diamonds Are Forever;
Bitcoin is Ephemeral

Bitcoin has an expiration date. It might not be for many years, but there will be a time when another currency overtakes Bitcoin. Bitcoin can and will be replaced by something better. It might be tomorrow. This is made even more likely by the fact that Bitcoin can so easily be traded into another cryptocurrency. There is little friction involved in exiting Bitcoin for another cryptocurrency. Most of the friction in a Bitcoin-based interaction is in moving from fiat money into Bitcoin and from Bitcoin into fiat money.

Don't be bothered by the fact that Bitcoin has an expiration date. Accept it and plan for a way to transition into the latest when that day comes. You are involved with the latest today; nothing is stopping you from being on the cutting edge when that transition out of Bitcoin starts to take place. The transition out of Bitcoin will be a complicated process for some – the timing, the change in concept, knowing where to and how to transition most cost-effectively. Those are issues many involved in Bitcoin will need to deal with. There will be money made by those who can simplify that process. Maybe you will be the entrepreneur credited with singlehandedly making the transition out of Bitcoin simpler for others.

From where we stand, the future of the Bitcoin protocol and the concept of cryptocurrencies is long and bright. Some people name the newest song an instant classic, or the newest technology a technology that will forever be part of our lives. Caught in the moment, such predictions are seldom accurate. Even the most well-regarded futurists are wrong on almost every prediction when they try to forecast a mere twenty years out. Forecasting the future is difficult. It is apparent that there is a market for a method of transaction that fits the decentralized nature of Bitcoin and can operate outside of existing financial structures. When government steps aside in such times of need, the free market thrives. When government intervenes in times of need, the black market thrives. At this moment of need, as long as Bitcoin remains the best, it will be the solution. This is of course an obvious statement. The second clause of course follows the first clause. That's how it tends to work, though, in a free-market environment.

I understand the excitement around the idea that Bitcoin is forever, that Bitcoin is the new paradigm. If we zoom out the microscope, it seems more likely that cryptocurrencies and cryptographic protocols reducing the need for third-party trust are likely a new paradigm. Bitcoin is a segment of that movement and currently the most important leader in that process. Cryptocurrencies will be a part of this shifting landscape for the foreseeable future.

There is good reason to focus development on one protocol right now: it allows an excited community of entrepreneurs to cooperate more easily towards solving the challenges that exist in that space. Along those lines, there is benefit to operating as if Bitcoin were the only option. A key reason is that it allows greater focus for the Bitcoin community.

Bitcoin Can Be Stopped — Maybe? Cryptocurrencies Can't

Plenty of commodities traders claim to notice "painted charts" where markets are moved intentionally by some powerful force. These are large markets, not puny markets like the Bitcoin market. When a contract trades with aggressive downward volatility, it becomes clear who has "strong hands" and who has "weak hands." Strong hands, for example, might be an investor with an unleveraged long-term bullish position that he, with discipline, sells off a portion of on upward moves and buys back on downward moves.

A big bank or a money-printing government can pound Bitcoin out of the weak hands so severely that Bitcoin will lose any recognition as an investment. Volatile price movements that push an investment vehicle out of weak hands are a common occurrence. This would be an easy way to cause damage to Bitcoin the currency. Enough movement like that and few people with weak hands will want to touch Bitcoin the currency.

Trades intended to influence the market are a common occurrence across investment classes. It would be naive to assume Bitcoin will not be subject to the same moves by outsiders seeking to intentionally move the Bitcoin market.

Fans of fringe political candidates know most intimately that another method of depreciating the value of a newsworthy occurrence, such as the growth of Bitcoin, is to simply attack it in the media. Furthermore, what the media gives, the media can take away. Organic growth in popularity builds stable bases. Sudden publicity builds unstable bases. Media attacks could harm Bitcoin. Weak hands occur in the media world as well, just as they do in the investment world. They are the fair-weather fans with no compass, no conviction guiding their decisions. Usually, if the media has not brought positive publicity, then its negative publicity has little effect. If the media did not bring the weak hands into Bitcoin then it can't chase the weak hands from Bitcoin.

Bitcoin has been slandered and attacked time and again and some would say it has shown resilience. Maybe that means Bitcoin is impervious to media attacks. It probably doesn't mean that though. There are few guarantees in investments. Experienced bull market traders know that the market will always bounce back until it doesn't.

The protocol that underlies Bitcoin and the concept of cryptocurrencies is more important and lasting than mere price fluctuations.

Of course, you understand that the price of Bitcoin against other forex instruments has little to do with the potential of the Bitcoin protocol, even in a bubble situation.

Bubble

Keep in mind that a bubble can't be identified until after it has grown and popped. We have tremendous liquidity in the world currency markets. Conditions are ripe for a bubble. Prepare yourself for the reality that Bitcoin could again trade at a dollar. If you do not consider that to be possible, even remotely possible, please revisit the history of bubbles and think through your philosophy toward Bitcoin further. Anything is possible. How likely you find it to be is another question.

If Bitcoin did trade at a dollar, would you be chased away? Would you be chased away from one of the greatest technologies to affect human interaction on a worldwide scale just because you lost some money in an investment? Would you sour on Bitcoin, when in fact you should just sour on your own illogical disconnect between risk and reward that hamstrings your investment goals?

If so, that would be sad. It shouldn't sour you or anyone else to the potential of the Bitcoin protocol and *it is after all the Bitcoin protocol and not the value of Bitcoin as a currency that we should be so excited about.*

Store Of Value

Bitcoin is subject to wild price swings. An adventurous process of price discovery is taking place. Throughout the history of man, items that are new or perceived to be new underwent wild price swings. Swampside real estate, railroads, tulips, Internet stocks, land along the Mississippi, and Bitcoin are some examples.

Bitcoin provides safety from government confiscation and prevents devaluation of currency from inflation. In those ways it is a good store of value. As it undergoes this period of price discovery, these wild fluctuations prevent Bitcoin from being the even better store of value that it may one day become. In time, the fluctuations may work themselves out and Bitcoin might assume a role as a stable store of value. Today it is not that.

Bitcoin Is Not Supremely Secure

Bitcoin relies on SHA-256. SHA-256 was developed by the NSA and released for public use. The NSA has long waged a war on encryption. The NSA war on encryption has been taking place since before SHA-256 was released by the NSA.

All encryption systems are impervious until they aren't. Quantum computers will become a reality one day. Quantum computers will cause Bitcoin to be less secure. Other technologies not yet thought of will also become a reality.

Addressing a need for an even better encryption system is an issue Bitcoin entrepreneurs may find themselves dealing with. Rising to that challenge should not be difficult for the innovative and energetic community working in the Bitcoin space.

Bitcoin May Never Be
Widely Adopted

I say this as a statement of downside risk. Bitcoin might never catch on. Look at the crudeness of early technologies; they often start out as a spark of insight jotted on a scrap of paper, then become a prototype in various stages before they are consumer-facing. Many products do not take their highest and best form in the hands of the original designer. Many producers refine already good products, putting out many different versions into a marketplace that chooses what it likes so viciously that some variants quickly disappear. These powerful forces shape a great deal of the world around us.

Bitcoin might not make it through that process. Its use as a currency might never catch on. Its protocol might be too flawed to be of use for anything. Its use as an investment vehicle might prove inferior to other financial products.

The market might reject it. No one can say for sure. If it were a sure thing, Warren Buffett and Charlie Munger would be buyers instead of refusing to even dignify the existence of Bitcoin with even a single logical sentence. Silence is all it gets from the Oracle of Omaha. There are so many sure things in the world that the smart money tends to stay away from investments that aren't sure things.

All technologies, new products, services, ideas start out a brutish figure compared to what they eventually become before catching on. In its fifth year, Bitcoin has come a long way. The Internet took decades to become big and still finds detractors far and wide for the smooth information transfer system that was once little more than a way for researchers to send numbers to each other. Of course, at its core, the Internet remains nothing more than the back-and-forth transmission of ones and zeroes. The layers of technology built around that method of transmitting ones and zeroes make the Internet accessible to anyone in the world. That took decades.

In these five years, a vast and powerful peer-to-peer network has ironed out difficulties in the Bitcoin protocol and is already developing products and services meant to allow the world to better interface with Bitcoin and the Bitcoin protocol.

It's difficult to predict the future and impossible to know what will become of Bitcoin. Perhaps it too, like the Internet, will take decades to catch on. Since the Bitcoin protocol operates using the communication framework of the Internet, this scenario is unlikely. Chances are it will catch on more quickly than the Internet did. After all, so many communicational issues with the network have already been dealt with.

It's not entirely fair, therefore, to compare Bitcoin to the arduous decades-long development we've seen so far with the Internet. Bitcoin being built upon the Internet means that the ground it needs to cover in order to be more widely accepted and function more flawlessly is significantly reduced. From that perspective, Bitcoin builds on some forty years of modern cryptography. This latest manifestation of cryptography solves problems that allow it a bright future in a way that other cryptographic protocols had not provided for.

Maybe Bitcoin as a currency in its current form will never be widely adopted. Maybe. The many entrepreneurial activities currently taking place around Bitcoin make for a constantly changing Bitcoin environment that is likely to grow, be adopted, and expand around the globe.

Snapshots into the Bitcoin ecosystem in a variety of cities around the world show intensive brainpower and resources being attracted into this ecosystem, a scenario that makes it vastly more likely Bitcoin will have an impact on world commerce, propelled by the excitement of such energy.

I have a great deal of confidence that Bitcoin will become big and change aspects of life that no one would ever have dreamed might be changed.

It will be succeeded by other cryptocurrencies and cryptotechnologies providing additional opportunities that those active in developing the Bitcoin space will be most capable of taking advantage of. All of this will have many layers built upon it to make it more functional. The upside is unimaginable. Bitcoin and other cryptographic protocols can become the most significant technological change any of us have ever known in our lifetimes.

To refuse to entertain what the possible downside risk of a Bitcoin investment is should not sit well with any seasoned investor. Any new investor unwilling to ask the tough questions seasoned investors ask should reflect on whether they are needlessly rein-venting the wheel. Please remember the Bitcoin protocol does not deserve your op-probrium when an unexamined investment leaves you feeling burnt.

Calling Out Liars

It's hard sometimes, but important, to call out people for telling lies. I'd like to ask you to do that. Doing so improves the environment around Bitcoin. Just because you think Bitcoin is awesome does not mean you need to tolerate hollow cheerleading or brazen lies. Bitcoin has some serious problems that need resolving for it to grow more useful. Ignoring those flaws serves few people.

In fact, more than anyone, these pro-Bitcoin lies seem to be beneficial to those who would prefer to see Bitcoin fail, because they hamper Bitcoin's development and harm the credibility of anyone advocating for Bitcoin. Some Bitcoin proponents get offended by those making unkind comments about Bitcoin.

Getting offended and encouraging others to cautiously quiet down rather than point out a flaw diminishes the quality of the discussion surrounding Bitcoin and will inevitably diminish the potential of Bitcoin. Pointing out truthful flaws while keeping an upbeat attitude toward Bitcoin and being rigorous about how to address those flaws is a healthier place for a community of developers to find themselves.

Getting Offended By Anti-Bitcoin Trolls

I recently heard a gentleman razzing a member of the Bitcoin community by saying, "What I really want to know is how I can short Bitcoin." The reaction to that was unpleasant. Bitcoin fell significantly over the next few days. As uncomfortable as it may have been to hear, shorting Bitcoin at that moment was the right trade. In the investment world, it is beneficial to listen to and entertain contrary opinions because they can shed light on the strengths and weaknesses of your own view of the market.

Getting offended by an exchange of opinions tends to show that you are insecure about your opinion or that you have something to prove. Neither of these options demonstrates impressive personal character, nor are they conducive to wise investing.

It's okay to hate on a troll a little. Just don't get too emotional about it; don't let it bother you. Keep your passions separate from ego and separate from your money making. Passion, money, and ego don't all fit nicely in the life of an individual. One of those aspects of life – usually money – gets chased away by the other two.

If you feel yourself getting offended by comments made to you about Bitcoin, it may be best to tone down your ego before you start losing money. While you're at it, you might be able to learn a few lessons by listening to a person who has essentially the exact opposite opinion to yours on a matter, especially if it's an investment matter.

Bitcoin Is Not Frictionless

A frictionless market is a trading environment without costs such as commission or taxes or other restraints to trading. Frictionless markets are theoretical. It is claimed by some that Bitcoin is frictionless – an inaccurate claim. Bitcoin certainly has promising advances that bring us closer to that frictionless market.

It is easy to send value from one Bitcoin wallet to another in the form of Bitcoin, whether that wallet is in the same room as you or on the other side of the world from you. That is most certainly convenient. A learning curve exists in that process and quite a bit of effort can be required to take Bitcoin to and from fiat currency.

As already discussed, Bitcoin is not a good store of value. Due to Bitcoin's price instability, there is a great deal of foreign exchange risk in using Bitcoin to transmit value since the transmission of Bitcoin from one wallet to another is not time-consuming, whereas the transmission out of Bitcoin into fiat currency can be.

This means that if Andrew (using US dollars) wants to pay Bertha (who wants British pounds), from the time Andrew buys Bitcoin with dollars, sends the Bitcoin to Bertha, and Bertha converts them to pounds, the value of the Bitcoin as measured in fiat could have changed. If this evens out – sometimes being up three percent, sometimes being down three percent – then everything would be okay with this scenario. It doesn't work that way though. Bitcoin is so volatile, there's a great rush for Andrew to hurry the Bitcoin to Bertha and for Bertha to hurry the Bitcoin into a more stable store of value – such as fiat.

If your digital currency is a worse store of value than central-bank-inflated fiat, then your digital currency is a pretty unstable store of value. Simply waiting until you finish lunch, or a subway ride, or – God forbid – receiving the Bitcoin payment in the middle of the night as you sleep, and not being able to transfer to fiat right away puts you at risk of losing ten or twenty percent. That's a mighty amount of friction on a transaction.

Business hours in London are 4:00 a.m. to noon in New York City, which are relatively inconvenient hours, but hours that we must abide by if every minute counts in a transaction. Part of the business day overlaps between those cities, making this more convenient. Being long Bitcoin is a lot like a trader being long a commodity contract.

A trader doesn't venture far from the pit or terminal when there's a position on, because there is so much volatility in a market that a leveraged position requires you to be ready to quickly get out of a position when it risks turning against you.

New York and London are very close, separated only by a common language and a few hours of air travel. Manila, for example, does not share business hours with New York. When the New York Stock Exchange is open, it's 10:30 p.m. to 5:00 a.m. in Manila, Singapore, and Beijing. In Tokyo, it's 11:30 p.m. to 6:00 a.m. These are not convenient times to be awake, waiting for Bitcoin to show up in a wallet and then trading it immediately for cash.

This volatility causes some limitations in using Bitcoin as a payment system. This is perhaps merely a kink that will in time be worked out. For the time being, it is a big kink. This brings us back to that issue of ten or twenty percent risk that could be associated with relying on Bitcoin as a store of value, whether for a few days or merely a few hours.

Depending on the industry, a ten or twenty percent increase in costs will put a company out of business; a ten or twenty percent increase in taxes would cause a factory to be shuttered and relocated to another jurisdiction. Ten or twenty percent is a great risk, and those numbers aren't even capped there. Intra-day Bitcoin can trade even more wildly than that.

Operating between Bitcoin and fiat – a necessary evil in a world economy that is not priced in Bitcoin – creates a great deal of friction. At present, this is friction that is built into Bitcoin by its very nature of being a free-market currency that is not backed by the government or the central bank of an industrialized country. This friction should be expected as consumers try to find the role of Bitcoin in the world market.

There are other sources of friction in Bitcoin transactions; for example, the above scenario does not take into account the friction between fiat currencies and Bitcoin caused by the various anti-money-laundering and know-your-customer compliances created by government or the onerous hurdles put up by banks, which happen to be hurdles often also caused by government.

Nor does it take into account the very long clearing time some Bitcoin firms impose on customers as part of their business model. The above example only looks at the smoothest possible scenario, in which Bitcoin is purchased for cash dollars, face to face, the trade is confirmed, sent from the US wallet to the British wallet, and then sold for cash pounds.

These less-than-ideal scenarios are precisely the types of situations that allow entrepreneurs to enter the market and add value by truly making Bitcoin a nearly frictionless method of transaction. If that issue of friction is not discussed frankly in the Bitcoin community, there is less opportunity to identify flaws and address them through the entrepreneurial process. At present, Bitcoin is not frictionless. It is far from frictionless – the opposite of frictionless. One day, Bitcoin might be nearly frictionless.

This Isn't Kickball, So I Don't Have To Pick A Side

While Bitcoin is sometimes lied about by its proponents, a group who tend to have high hopes and big dreams for the future, it is denounced widely by opponents. I would prefer to take a sober view of the world, and do not need to choose a team to be on. I'm not on any team.

If I had to count myself more impressed with one side or the other, it's those who dream big about what an increasingly great place the world can be, rather than those with a dour gloom-and-doom prediction of how unlikely change is and how terrible change would be anyway if it even occurred.

Having lived through an age made so much better by entrepreneurs and consumers interacting in a free market, I have great optimism for the many challenges in life that can be overcome by allowing those same market interactions to work their magic. This isn't rocket science.

There's a lot of gloom-and-doom in the world pointed at this protocol that seeks to revolutionize how we interact with each other financially.

Bitcoin – A Hard-Hearted Harbinger Of Crime

The common narrative about Bitcoin says that it invites criminal elements because of its anonymity. The implication is that, because bad things are done by people using Bitcoin, then Bitcoin, too, is a bad thing. According to some narratives, Bitcoin should even be banned, it is so bad.

The currency that is most used for crime is the Federal Reserve Note, the US dollar. It is the most laundered currency. It is the most sought-after currency in criminal events worldwide. It's so important that the majority of dollars are believed to circulate outside of the United States. Whenever there is a crime, the US dollar is the currency that is most often caught up in that crime.

Many crimes are motivated by or have some monetary component. The following is an abbreviated list of crimes in which US dollars are the most commonly involved currency worldwide: money laundering; arms trafficking; human trafficking; khat trafficking; funding militias; piracy on the high seas; pirate financing; migrant smuggling; forgery; personation; impersonation; electioneering; voluntary manslaughter; forcible rape; aggravated assault; simple assault; robbery; burglary; buggery; arson; larceny; theft; grand theft auto; war crimes; forced disappearance; genocide; piracy; assassination; sexual slavery; regular slavery; waging a war of aggression; war crimes; embezzlement; sabotage; murder; battery; manslaughter; dueling; vehicular homicide; tax evasion; fraud; the manufacture, sale, distribution, or possession with intent to distribute of certain types and quantities of illegal drugs; regicide; grand larceny; vandalism; gambling; treason; kidnapping; obstruction of justice; perjury; check fraud; child pornography; mail tampering; violating parole; threatening an official; breaking and entering of a dwelling house at night with the intent to commit larceny, assault and battery, or any felony therein; breaking and entering with further criminal intent; possession of a deadly weapon; driving while intoxicated; cyber bullying; assisted suicide; kidnapping; insurance fraud; identity theft; unlawful restraint; aiding and abetting a crime; debit card fraud; drug cultivation and manufacture; extortion; indecent exposure; racketeering; securities fraud; bribery; motor vehicle arson; resisting arrest; motor vehicle harassment; disorderly conduct; motor vehicle sabotage; money laundering; laundering money while operating a motor vehicle; unsworn falsification; conspiring to commit treason; discussing treasonous acts while operating a motor vehicle; wire fraud; conspiracy; extortion; racketeering; making false statements to insurance regulators; homosexual lewd conduct; heterosexual lewd conduct; lewd conduct in a government building; lewd conduct in the Oval Office; use and possession of embargoed Cuban products by a US national in government buildings; obstruction of justice and solicitation of illegal pornography; bank fraud; unlawful representation of service in the US armed forces; fraudulently filling out absentee ballots for residents of nursing homes; filing false disclosure forms in order to hide unauthorized income; accepting bribes; impersonating an officer; impersonating a member of the opposite sex online;

impersonating a priest; impersonating a public servant; impersonating with intent to defraud.

Even minor legal infractions such as jaywalking, when done for financial reasons, are more likely to involve the US dollar than any other currency. Following the same reason, one might wonder if jaywalking might no longer exist if the US dollar were simply banned.

Bitcoin – A Harbinger Of Theft

Some go after Bitcoin because it is the subject of theft. US dollars are the most widely stolen currency in value terms. Is that a reason to ban the dollar? Major artwork is widely stolen, jewels are stolen, both containing very compact stores of value, in highly publicized stories. Does that mean the works of da Vinci should just be taken out back and burned, and the Louvre stripped of its art and made into a shelter for African refugees? No, of course not; that would be preposterous. In fact, there's something sexy about the thefts of these items that are dense with value. Such drama may actually increase our appreciation of these high-value items. Movies are even made about them in which the thieves always end up having sculpted, fatless bodies.

High-value Bitcoin thefts will achieve the same status. For some they already have. Angry hackers, burned by other hackers, chase their perpetrator through cyberspace, tracking their movements, busting through all manners of defenses, watching their Bitcoin travel through the Blockchain, watching their hard work get tumbled into oblivion, and then tracking it through the tumbler as those wallets bleed, sending six hundred sixty-six Satoshis to their perpetrator's new wallet, just to say, "I'm watching you," and then posting that wallet key publicly for others to send angry messages to – a community of hackers saying, "We're watching you" to the perpetrator. Or, who knows, maybe a few will commend the hacker with messages like, "Brilliant heist!" This is fascinating stuff – the stuff movies are made of.

Anything electronic with access to the Internet is always at risk. Big banks know that a customer's assets might be inconvenient for the customer to reach in a "cold" account, but that by being offline, that account is free from theft through the Internet. Whenever an account is left "hot," is left online, anyone should realize the folly of trusting that such assets are secure. The hacking aficionado is likely to one day commend his hacker for so artfully parting him from his money. Even in being duped can there be beauty. Burn the da Vincis? Ban Bitcoin? Shutter the Louvre? That all sounds foolish.

The US Dollar – Accepted By More Dictators Than Any Other Currency Worldwide

US dollars are so important to the drug trade that there's cocaine all over our money. According to results of a study done at the University of Illinois, Chicago, 92.8 percent of publicly circulated Federal Reserve Notes tested positive for trace amounts of cocaine. A University of Massachusetts Dartmouth study showed one hundred percent of bills in circulation in large American cities tested positive for cocaine, while only sixty-seven to eighty-seven percent of dollars in smaller cities tested positive. In February 2012, a gas station in Ann Arbor, Michigan was shut down and three employees were taken to hospital after handling money that had been contaminated in a meth lab.

On top of that, money is disgustingly dirty. Researchers involved in a 2002 study published in the *Southern Medical Journal* found that ninety-four percent of Federal Reserve Notes in circulation have potentially disease-causing pathogens such as pneumonia causing bacteria and staphylococcus aureus. E. coli, shigella, and detectable amounts of fecal matter are commonly present on bills.

In addition to the Federal Reserve Notes being dirty, disease carrying, and contaminated with drugs, it's worth noting that Bitcoin is not the preferred currency of dictators. The US dollar is. Just one example is that man who Americans have loved to hate these last twenty-five years, a man who Americans have come to view as the Hitler of his own corner of the world – Saddam Hussein. This man has been perceived so negatively since

9/11 that polls have shown anywhere from seventy percent (in 2003) to a third of Americans (today) believing that Saddam Hussein was personally involved in the attacks. Yes, the most evil man of the last twenty-five years has been falsely accused of being a collaborator of the most evil man of the last fifteen years – bin Laden. Here are some anecdotes involving that villain and the Federal Reserve Notes – preferred by more dictators around the world than any other currency.

April 2003, some $650 million in $100 bills are found in a residential area of Baghdad behind a false wall of a residence. In the same area, more than $100 million was found in an animal kennel. The bills were brand new and sequential with markings from the Federal Reserve Banks of New York, Boston, and Philadelphia.

This treasure trove was believed to belong to Saddam Hussein.

December 13, 2003, as part of Operation Red Dawn, the US Military sought out Saddam Hussein in two locations in Ad-Dawr near Tikrit, Iraq, where they believed they might find him, but he ends up not being at either. Later that day, they find Hussein in a nearby hole in possession of 750,000 US dollars.

August 7, 2007, $20 billion denominated in $100 bills spread across two hundred pallets were being held at Moscow's Sheremetyevo Airport, after being seen arriving from Frankfurt, Germany. The money is believed to have belonged to the late Saddam Hussein.

Dictators love US dollars. Bad guys everywhere are into them. Criminals favor them over other currencies. The dollar is the world's reserve currency. We can sit and quibble over whether ninety percent or only eighty percent of dictators, criminals, and miscellaneous fiends prefer the US dollar. It should be clear that Bitcoin is not the true choice of the criminally minded. The US dollar is. Should we ban the US dollar to undermine dictators? Is the US dollar the cause of oppressive regimes? Of course not.

Bitcoin Is A Symbol for Something Greater: A World Without Central Banking

It's easy to look at a volatile chart and laugh at how terrifying Bitcoin is and how only fools would be involved in anything so unpredictably volatile. It's easy to look at the many Bitcoin exchanges and to talk about how the exchanges can't even agree on a buy and sell price for Bitcoin.

It's easy to ignore the currency most commonly used for paying for illicit activity – the US dollar – and to focus instead on the fact that Bitcoin, just like every other currency that has ever existed, is used to pay for illicit activity. The most stolen money on the planet is the US dollar, a convenient fact to ignore as Bitcoin theft is focused on.

All of that is a distraction, however, from what Bitcoin really is. It is of course a currency. Under that is the very important Bitcoin protocol. The protocol is confusing to understand. It takes some people a great deal of study to really have a command of the protocol. In contrast, any second grader can read a Bitcoin forex chart and write an article attacking its volatility.

More than a currency, Bitcoin is a symbol of something greater: a world without central banking. It portends a world without a need for the (sometimes burdensome) level of (often ineffective) government intrusion we've grown used to. Part of the beauty of Bitcoin is that no one person has any idea where this experiment will lead. This is true for every free-market experiment. If that weren't the case, central planning would work a lot more smoothly.

As consumers and entrepreneurs interact, they will come to find uses for the Bitcoin protocol that no one, to date, has ever considered. What is clear is that some of the innovative energy that was focused on revolutionizing communication through the Internet is now focused on using Bitcoin and other cryptocurrency protocols to revolutionize financial dealings.

Bitcoin Should Be Used To Buy Drugs

Some in the Bitcoin space are apologetic about the criminal activity that has occurred or can occur using Bitcoin. I cringe when I hear such moralizing tied up with this technology. It's pathetic. It's often done as an attempt to sway moderate American society towards Bitcoin by feigning interest in upholding a given set of morals. The nature of human beings welcomes illicit activity. I am willing to wager that every freely traded currency in existence is used in some form of illicit activity.

Cash is incredibly easy to make anonymous and cash transactions are permanently un-traceable, something that Bitcoin is unable to promise at this time since the Blockchain permanently records every transaction ever conducted with Bitcoin.

Bitcoin allows value to travel great distances more easily outside of traditional banking channels, which is certainly easier than trans-porting cash across borders and distances. These do not make for an irresistible invitation to engage in prurient behavior. Eventually there will be technology available that can decrypt these transmissions that have been recorded and broadcast for all to see. Using today's available technology, Bitcoin can be used anonymously.

To anyone who appreciates anonymous transactions, however, Bitcoin may appear to be the opposite: an accounting of people who desire secrecy. Again, flaws like this are not detrimental, especially in such an active entrepreneurial environment. The flaws, however, should be discussed honestly, in order to help improve the shortcomings.

In some ways cash is superior for quiet transactions; in other ways Bitcoin is superior. One such quiet transaction might be the purchase of illegal drugs. The purchase of illegal drugs is so intertwined with the US dollar that nine out of ten Federal Reserve Notes, as previously pointed out, have traces of cocaine on them. So, if any currency should be credited with expanding the drug trade, it should be the US dollar.

Even if the roles were reversed, however, what would be so bad about that? What is so bad about using money to buy drugs?

What's wrong with using Bitcoin to buy drugs? Should someone who had nothing to do with the purchase be publicly apologetic? That doesn't make much sense. A pleasant aspect of Bitcoin is that when combined with the worldwide computer network we have, it makes black markets more accessible, even from the other side of the world.

It is morally appropriate for a government to allow someone to peacefully put what he or she wants in his or her own body. If Bitcoin makes it easier to subvert immoral drug laws and to allow individuals to find peaceful recreation however they see fit, then Bitcoin holds a morally superior position. Bitcoin should be used to buy drugs.

Illegal drugs obviously do cause damage to society. Criminalizing their use and imprisoning victims of drug addiction does even more damage. This is so true that it's entirely fair to call the War on Drugs immoral. Minority communities are disproportionately affected by the War on Drugs, further adding to the immoral enforcement where the purported "cure" does more damage than the disease.

Drugs aren't good. I have no dreamy illusions about expanding my mind by putting junk in my body. Even worse than drugs is the War on Drugs. If Bitcoin allows the immoral and damaging War on Drugs to be further subverted, then that's a morally superior position held by Bitcoin. Perhaps it's worth repeating that point once more: *Bitcoin should be used to buy drugs. Encouraging the purchase of drugs with Bitcoin is in fact the moral thing to do.*

The only reason to apologize for Bitcoin's use in the purchase of illegal drugs is to appease someone who is threatened by the realization that the War on Drugs is a miserable failure that causes a great deal more pain than it prevents. That pandering is pathetic for someone operating on the cutting edge of society.

Society will catch up. But that issue is far beyond the point. Why should a third party appear apologetic for anything, sometimes even horrific things, that are paid for with any currency? Silliness. Some in the Bitcoin community play right into this silliness. Toughen up.

Please Do Your Laundry
At Least Once A Week

There's a term that is often challenged as being naughty, without being questioned. Dirty money is laundered to make it appear clean. As any child who listens to his mother knows, money is really, really dirty and is never clean. There is the idea, however, that anyone moving money around to obscure the original source of that money is doing something bad. There was a time where that was known as privacy in America.

Imagine how silly it would sound if protestors suddenly appeared outside a courthouse or at the local diet, calling for great protection for money launderers. Ridiculous – right? It shouldn't be, though. Government, especially the US Government, has taken it upon themselves to be able to track every financial transaction that takes place.

This is totally contrary to the idea of privacy. It is just another example of the long-held concept that government is the most forcefully intrusive entity that infringes on our privacy.

From the perspective of a government like that, cash is their enemy, because cash is secretive. Bitcoin is their enemy, because Bitcoin is secretive. Bitcoin, done a little differently, has the potential to be the Federal Government's ally in this war on privacy because it has a record of every transaction ever undertaken. Link the pseudonyms to the identities of the Bitcoin users and the Block-chain becomes an eavesdropping govern-ment's dream. Without that, Bitcoin is an enemy to the government because it affords secrecy to individuals.

The concept of secrecy has been turned on its head. Governments declare significant amounts of their activity secret, illegal to disclose or otherwise talk about. At the same time, all private activity done by the individual is to be laid bare like an open book for the government to inspect at will.

If for any reason a person seeks privacy, that person is immediately suspect – why would you desire privacy unless you were doing something worth hiding? That question is a question that would only be posed by some-one who doesn't understand privacy. Privacy from government intrusion is a feeling of comfort that anyone is afforded unless there is clear evidence that the person has done something wrong.

Money laundering, encrypting communication, not volunteering your personal papers to any government entity that feels like taking a peek is as American as the US Constitution. *Money laundering is as American as the US Constitution.*

It says a great deal about how little Americans value privacy when even a single politician feels comfortable denouncing the concept of money laundering in public. Anyone who desires private financial records deserves private financial records that the US Government will never be able to access.

That's one of the dreams of Bitcoin. That's something that was able to come about only because the US Government became so egregious with its behavior that enough people said, "How do we combat these powerful untrustworthy institutions that have taken center stage in our lives?"

One answer is that we make government irrelevant. Bitcoin is a step on the path toward making government irrelevant. Deep down, I despise anyone who takes a soap box at a hearing about Bitcoin and wags their finger at how evil it is. But then, I take a step back and smile.

That person, that talented person who chose to become a bureaucrat instead of doing something beautiful with his life – that person does not matter. That person, in choosing to be a bureaucrat, deemed himself and his life largely irrelevant.

Two generations ago he may have mattered to the general public. In this century, he matters little, and by century's close he will matter not at all. You can credit technology for that. You can credit developments in Bitcoin.

Let me let you in on a little secret, though: there are people in the world to whom he's never mattered, because they've never accepted as legitimate the authority of someone like that. There are people like that who have lived free lives with free minds in every age and in every place.

Valuable items are always in demand at a price that is lower than the asking price. It is part of what gives them value. That is the nature of anything valuable. Saying that Bitcoin should somehow be banned because it invites theft is simply illogical. It would be as illogical as avoiding theft by shuttering the Louvre or taking the Mona Lisa out back to be burned. Should one really be shocked that media coverage or statements made by government officials are both illogical and ages behind any trend taking place?

Large Parts Of The Financial Sector Can Become Obsolete Thanks To Bitcoin

At the basis of the Bitcoin protocol is a desire to replace unearned trust with cryptography. Until now, to function financially you had to trust a great number of vendors who you did not personally know. A concept behind Bitcoin is that if all software used is open-source, and you have a solid enough understanding of the software to be able to verify its veracity, then you do not need to trust anyone to assure you that the software is solid software.

These are two big "ifs" that are about to follow, ifs that are difficult to ensure, but for which the logic is sound. Those who develop the technology that helps us reach this goal have achieved something admirable for the world. If all encryptions are secure and open-source, and your analysis of the encryptions sound, then your funds are secure. Secure, transparent software replaces a great deal of the trust required in an interaction.

Using a series of simple if-then commands, Bitcoin can replace a large array of financial services that also, in essence, operate according to if-then commands. There are more details to this, but essentially, any institution and any interaction that requires our unearned trust today can plausibly be replaced by some form of Bitcoin-based transaction. In line with the nature of entrepreneurship, I have no idea how this will be accomplished. I know, however, that, with the right incentives in the market, it will.

Bitcoin Is A Waste Of Electricity

Are you kidding me? How many kilowatts are being spent on watching the Kardashians right now, yet you are wasting precious resources to criticize Bitcoin, a system that will allow 2.5 billion people to be banked for the first time in their lives, will bring the widespread happiness of a world free-market financial system, and will free the entire planet of the very stringent banking industry that we find ourselves saddled with.

What a foolish concept it is to denounce Bitcoin for not being green enough or for leaving too big a carbon footprint. The people who pay for the electricity that comes out of the wall should be able to use the electricity any way they want. For those who see the world purely in terms of how big of a carbon footprint exists, you probably are too big of a ninny to be reading this book. In case there are such readers, I will point out an important upside.

There do not seem to be very credible measures of how much energy Bitcoin presently uses. I agree; a lot of power is used to operate the Bitcoin network, which as of late November 2013 had accomplished the feat of being two hundred and fifty-six times faster than the world's five hundred fastest supercomputers combined. It's an energy-intensive process.

Much of America was once heated using coal, a rather ecologically unfriendly energy source, especially when it is coming out of thousands of chimneys in an urban area, instead of a central chimney with effective scrubbers. It was not for reasons of being green that the switch happened away from coal for home heating; simple economics made coal a less attractive option.

It may be comforting to know that in time, Bitcoin mining, like virtually every technology, will likely become even more efficient. The market will push for greater efficiency and lower costs in mining Bitcoin. This is another of those problems that will be solved by the interplay between consumers and entrepreneurs operating in the free market. If consumers desire less electrically intense ways to confirm Bitcoin transactions, then they will have them. *Bitcoin does use a lot of electricity. It is also a good use of a lot of electricity.*

The Unbanked

According to the FDIC, ten percent of US households have no checking account, twenty-nine percent have no savings account, eight percent – nearly ten million households – are "unbanked." Forty-three million adults are unbanked and use non-bank money orders or check-cashing services, payday loans, and rent-to-own agreements or pawnshops on a regular basis.

Blacks, Hispanics, and Native Americans are most likely to be underbanked. Twenty-five million American adults have no credit score, according to Mission Asset Fund. According to McKinsey and Company, 2.5 billion, over half of the world's adult population, do not use formal or semi-formal banking services to save money. Literally half the world is unbanked.

The ability to bank opens up doors and is yet another example of how Bitcoin operating in a free market is a tool of social justice. This is not "social justice" the way it is commonly used. That common use makes the judgment call that government should choose winners and losers.

Social justice as it pertains to Bitcoin is a more accurate use of the word. Bitcoin helps create a world with more possibility, more opportunity, more chance to improve one's own situation in a variety of ways. Among those is putting up a tile and starting a business, or simply being able to buy and sell what one wants, or not having to worry about discriminatory government laws.

This is social justice. In fact, around the world, a common aspect of oppression is that the oppression tends to come from a government or that an oppressor uses government to validate the oppression.

Bitcoin creates a more socially just scenario, in part by weakening the role government can play in the lives of individuals. The importance of this to the world, and especially to those 2.5 billion unbanked, cannot be overstated. Traditional financial institutions have shown little interest in reaching this large segment of the population, who often resort to high banking fees and predatory lending environments. Bitcoin presents a possible alternative to this system.

The Sheer Joy Of Humanity When It Finds A Way To Cooperate En Masse

Imagine all the markets. Will you be the first to set up a functioning microbank between the Cubans of Havana and the Cubans of Miami? Or the Ethiopians of Addis Ababa and Washington DC? Ecuadorians of Quito and New York?

There are many places with strong concentrations of expatriates from a specific country that have a need to communicate with their ancestral lands, like the Iranians of Tehran and Los Angeles, the Senegalese of Dakar and New York, the Poles of Warsaw and Chicago, the Ukrainians of Kiev and Philadelphia, the Albanians of Tirana and Patterson, the Chinese of Beijing and San Francisco, the Nigeriens of Niamey and Houston, the Indians of New Delhi and Oakland, the Russians of Moscow and Highland Park, the Congolese of Kinshasa, Brazzaville, and Boston, the Sudanese of Juba, Khartoum and Omaha, the Hmong of Hanoi, Vientiane, and Wausau, the Hungarians of Budapest and Cleveland, or the Czechs of Prague and West, Texas.

There's a world of people separated from their ancestral lands who would like to have afforded to them the many varieties of communication – from speaking to and seeing each other over the Internet, to having a pocket blow up from text messaging back and forth in a second language, to sending monetary gifts cheaply and in an instant.

Rebuilding those relationships can be very rewarding. At the same time, when a person with some disposable income to invest re-establishes those contacts, that person has an entirely new investment realm opened up to him or her.

Imagine the good that will be done. Imagine the investments that can be made in humans and human potential.

I'm probably not going to invest in Moldova. The bank on the corner probably isn't going to start microbanking in Algeria, or guarantee a loan in occupied Tibet; however, immigrants who have come to the US from those places and made money may be very interested in investing in junk-bond countries with the likely result of greater rates of return.

They are the most natural choice for investments like that. What may seem to some as a high-risk junk-bond country may be seen by them as a high-return investment that needs someone who understands the culture in order to better help guide the project to fruition. That's instant value added by that investor. Being so comfortable between the two countries, they are the natural bridge.

As financial instruments develop, needing a decreasing amount of trust, while increasing the potential flow of investment capital, business financing like this will increasingly become an option. Later stage investors will enter such markets, following the lead of the early stage investors who, with their very presence and desire to make an investment with a strong return, helped an even greater sense of professionalism develop in their ancestral lands.

Entrepreneurs will come up with new methods of making this process more effective. Lives of people on both sides of this transaction will change as they do business with each other in a way never before seen. The upside potential is limitless.

NAFTA, CAFTA, GATT, and the WTO are bullshit. They do little for free trade. They benefit well-connected multinationals disproportionately. They are the opposite of free trade. Bitcoin, Silk Roads, the Internet open the world up to uninhibited worldwide free trade. Imagine what that unprecedented concept would even mean.

We are reaching an age where all people from anywhere in the world can receive educational instruction from the finest schools without leaving home, where anyone can interact with anyone else as employer, contractor, partner, vendor without ever having met each other face to face, where no government has the power to control the interaction. There will literally be nothing insurmountable stopping anyone in the world from reaching their dreams.

We have no fathomable way to grasp the human potential that is about to be released, potential that never before had a chance to work cooperatively on this scale – and to add further energy to that, it is human potential motivated by passion and profit.

Banking to 2.5 billion people is nice – that's room for a lot of business. When will you figure out a way to get in? Why not sit down with a pad of paper and scratch out ideas right now? What else would you do if you suddenly realized seven billion people were waiting to buy your product and that no government was powerful enough to stop it? Imagine the problems you could solve. Imagine all the people you could help. Why not get started right now?

Governments Will Crush Bitcoin

That's not really how Washington, DC works. People unfamiliar with the intimate workings of government generally default to the belief that something sinister is afoot. More often incompetence explains governmental action.

Some in DC would love to make the world a better place for all. More often than not they aren't smart enough to know how to make that happen.

Sir John Cowperthwaite became the financial secretary (1961-1971) of an economically devastated Hong Kong, insisting government step out of the way and that government intervention be as minimal as possible, as a way to spur innovation, growth, and prosperity for the people. His policies of stepping aside to allow the economy to function helped make it the most economically free economy in the world.

Hong Kong was left in a shambles post-World War II, following the Japanese occupation. A million penniless refugees arrived there after the 1949 communist takeover of China. Hong Kong had no natural resources and had to import its own food, making a successful turnaround appear quite unlikely.

Cowperthwaite said about the success that came out of this process, "I did very little. All I did was to try to prevent some of the things that might undo it." He shunned taxes; personal taxes never rose over fifteen percent.

No government borrowing, no tariffs, no subsidies. Even today Hong Kong has no VAT, no sales tax, no interest on capital gains, and a top personal tax rate of fifteen percent. Cowperthwaite refused special benefits to businesses and would not allow any but the most rudimentary economic data to be collected on the colony. He was certain data would lead to government coming along and interfering with an economy that needed no interfering with.

These decisions to not intervene allowed him to oversee the period of Hong Kong's fastest economic growth. During Cowperthwaite's tenure, Hong Kong's exports grew by an average of nearly fourteen percent annually, wages doubled, and extreme poverty dropped from fifty to sixteen percent. In 1961, the average income was a quarter that of Britain; by 1991, average incomes in Hong Kong had surpassed those in Britain. These extreme laissez-faire economic policies turned this backward corner of the world into a world financial center. Hong Kong went from a mere trading post to an economic and manu-facturing hub.

"That government is best which governs least," wrote the enlightened Thoreau. Those in government desiring to do their best and smart enough to accomplish the best for their constituents would see to it that government would do the least. This is far from what government actually does. Government, most often out of incompetence and ignorance, is constantly seeking to intervene.

The incompetence and ignorance of govern-ment goes into many aspects of government. The theory goes that governments will crush anything that undermines their control over money and that absolutely no competition in this area is allowed. We must remember the incompetence and ignorance of government.

What a government official wants is seldom what the official gets.

If you doubt this, do yourself a favor and spend twelve miserable months working a government job for the highest-level government politician you can secure a position with. If that official were competent, government wouldn't be his or her choice. Most people will not require twelve months to comprehend the incompetence and ignorance of so many government officials. I've always found that self-perceived insurgents underestimate the vast vulnerabilities of their enemy, often to their own detriment. The thought that government will crush Bitcoin is bogus. Most opponents of Bitcoin stop the discussion right there.

How Do You Destroy
A Decentralized Network?

Let's look at the BitTorrent protocol as an example. Government increasingly came out against the black market in entertainment media, where consumers sought to exercise their property rights over DVDs, CDs, hard drives, paper, and ink the way they saw fit. Preventing an owner of a printer, ink, and paper from printing out a book is an infringement on the property of the printer, ink, and paper owner. That's clear.

Whether anyone can legitimately own an idea is less clear. Patents and copyrights are methods of using governmental control to prevent competition in a market. Few are helped by preventing competition and many are harmed. As the government became increasingly harsh in persecuting those who exercised those property rights, just people came up with increasingly clever techniques for dealing with the government persecution.

Out of this environment, BitTorrent arose. Governments were harshly persecuting anyone operating a centralized file-sharing service. The solution was simple: make it decentralized. Make it so decentralized that there was no way for anyone to put a stop to it. Had government been able to prevent a decentralized system like that, the government would have. Those who were paying attention in those days saw that any sizeable enough decentralized system is beyond the reach of government. Government has no effective means of forcing regulation on a decentralized, widely dispersed network, and definitely no effective means of shutting it down.

Pirate Bay has developed an even more decentralized concept by implementing a browser-based peer-to-peer network that they are beefing up to allow for local storage of network indexes. There's no central server even containing indexes.

Of the estimated two hundred and fifty million BitTorrent protocol users, as many as two hundred thousand have been brought into some legal battle. That's less than one-tenth of one percent of users. This number – two hundred thousand – is almost certainly a myth perpetrated by big-wig entertainment lawyers seeking to flex their inordinately small muscles. When what you have to show is tiny, you might feel a need to give a person a sales pitch before showing it off. Whatever legal battles have occurred have had virtually no negative impact on the BitTorrent system. It's thriving. It's strong. That's despite tremendous effort to block the system.

With lazy minds, or uninformed minds, it is glibly stated that government will shut down Bitcoin anytime it wants. In addition to the aforementioned arguments that decentralized networks can't be shut down by a government, there's an important issue about what exactly it means to shut down Bitcoin. As always, it is important to distinguish between Bitcoin the currency and Bitcoin the protocol. Bitcoin the currency can be somewhat easily attacked, and the price can be depressed through open-market operations.

The President of the US has at his disposal the Working Group on Financial Markets, formed on March 18, 1988 by Executive Order 12631, which has the authority to engage in open-market operations, even those that are not in the best interest of the American people.

Of course, any intervention in a free market is not in the interest of the American people. The group includes the following, or a designated representative of the following: Secretary of the Treasury; Chairman of the Federal Reserve; Chairman of the SEC; and Chairman of the CFTC. They are charged with "enhancing the integrity, efficiency, orderliness, and competitiveness of our nation's financial markets and protecting investor confidence."

Formed in response to the October 19, 1987 Black Monday crash, this group was put together to better coordinate governmental responses to market events. From a free-market perspective, this group exists only to limit the activity of the free market. Whatever mechanism they use, this group operates according to a mission that is anathema to a free market. A free market is necessary for the relationship between entrepreneur and consumer to thrive at its strongest level.

Bitcoin's price can be hurt by misinformed media attacks as well. Bitcoin's use as a currency can be depressed and illegalized. That will not stop it from being used, but it can drastically decrease the price and cause it to move out of weak hands. I see no indication at present that this will happen. Surely, this is a downside risk that should be considered. This action only affects Bitcoin the currency.

That is a very different issue than government bringing down Bitcoin. The very concept of government having any possible intervention that would bring down the Bitcoin protocol is a stretch since there are so many entrepreneurs currently operating in the cryptocurrency space.

Even if the underlying technology proved ineffective at doing its job, that would only leave an opportunity for entrepreneurs to step up and improve the existing technologies. *Anyone who says that government can bring down Bitcoin is simply expressing a deep-seated belief that centralized governmental power is superior and more effective than the strength and effectiveness of a decentralized free market.* I have the opposite belief, demonstrated to me time and again, that shows government can't beat a free market and must eventually fall in line behind it as the market leads the way in demonstrating what consumers truly want. This market discovery process sometimes takes a long period of time, sometimes a short period of time. Technology has sped up this process.

Surely there are ways that government can intervene to oppose the use of Bitcoin. At the end of the day, the Bitcoin protocol remains outside of government's reach, unless the Bitcoin community seeks to embrace the government.

Government's Time Has Passed

The weaklings of the Bitcoin industry denounce Silk Road. Why should anyone care if Silk Road is good or bad? The most significant currency in the world for criminal activity is the US dollar. Does that mean we should ban the US dollar? The existence of the Silk Roads of the world, the existence of the Bitcoins of the world is simply a sign that government's time has passed. Playing nice with government so they will give you your fill is a dated idea.

The thought is that if we allow government to be a part of all this – educate enough people about Bitcoin – then we will find a favorable regulatory environment. That sounds like a bunch of baloney. Majority rule is overrated. You are talking about a country that had a government-imposed telephone monopoly thirty-five years ago, had a government-imposed utility monopoly in every state, and a severe government-imposed airline oligopoly. After seeing the joy of a little more freedom, a large portion of those American people continue to demand healthcare monopolies, currency monopolies, and educational monopolies.

Perhaps one can forgive such people for not knowing the economics of the situation. It's not so easy to forgive someone for not knowing the economics of the situation and insisting on being vocal about it. As a mid-twentieth-century economist once pointed out:

"It is no crime to be ignorant of economics, which is, after all, a specialized discipline and one that most people consider to be a 'dismal science.' But it is totally irresponsible to have a loud and vociferous opinion on economic subjects while remaining in this state of ignorance."

This is the likely scenario that will continue. To ignore the existence of this trend would be naïve on the part of the Bitcoin community. Understandably, some seek to educate the voter and politician, to encourage a more friendly regulatory environment. The other option is to maybe throw up their hands and to admit their helplessness in the situation in which majority government is bound to always make the wrong decision almost as surely as if government's wrongness were a rule of nature.

It doesn't have to be that way though. So many in the Bitcoin community can lead by example. They can be the change they hope to see in the world. At the same time, there are some in Bitcoin who would much prefer to cater to the lowest common denominator and wait for the lowest common denominator to catch up. The truth of the matter is that they will never catch up. A great percentage of the population will always be far behind and a lot of them will vote and hold influential positions in government. That too is practically a rule of nature.

Play nicely with them and hope they won't regulate your gobbledygook play currency too much? That sounds like a terrible plan to me. Lead and sheep will follow. Those trying to convince you to stop leading, stop growing, stop developing, stop doing, and to instead spend your time teaching the unteachable and asking the sheep for permission are definitely part of the problem. Try tuning them out.

FASB And Bitcoin –
Methods Of Regulation

Some industries are regulated by governments. Health insurance is an example. The
most significant health insurance players
cooperate with government officials and even
help with drafting legislation. No matter how
burdensome the regulation, the regulation
helps them stay competitive against upstarts
seeking to serve their customer base more
effectively than the established players already
do. Relatively speaking, regulation is always a
greater burden on the upstart and the smaller
firm than it is on larger and more established
corporations. Healthcare, once entirely separate from health insurance, is another example
of a highly regulated industry. Like all other
government-regulated industries, poor service
and unresponsive consumer care are the norm

in healthcare, alongside rising prices and poor levels of innovation. Sadly, the cost of having this industry so heavily regulated by government is illness and death. This makes free-market healthcare so very important to pursue. It allows us to provide the amazing energy and motivation of the free market towards extending our own lives and the lives of those around us. It's sad to consider what human joy and potential has been stifled by healthcare regulators.

Some industries are regulated by the market. This seems to be the ideal method of regulation to allow for innovation and choice for consumers. The laptop you purchase today is much more powerful and perhaps even less expensive than the laptop you purchased two years ago. Competition is aggressive among manufacturers, and consumers are constantly testing and retesting what products are best, in an effort to exceed the best. Many computer makers have gone out of business, unable to deal with these aggressive market environments while, at the same time, consumers have increasingly come to get what we want from computer manufacturers. What was once an antiquated telephone on the wall in a telecommunications industry that was regulated to the point of monopoly is now combined with a computer in your pocket. The mere act of allowing the free market to work its magic dramatically speeds the pace of innovation. Allowing the free market to regulate the tech industry has been tremendously advantageous to consumers. We can credit these developments as being a natural result of the interaction that takes place between consumer and entrepreneur in a free-market environment.

Other industries tend to be regulated by the market, with some level of self-regulation. Plastic surgery is an example; so is LASIK eye surgery. These procedures get less expensive over time, contrary to the many other highly regulated areas of medicine. Through various methods of information exchange, new patients find out which doctors are good and which are bad. The bad doctors are ignored or go out of business. The good doctors are rewarded with new business. Doctors who perform badly enough may be punished by the medical boards under which they are licensed. This is an uncommon occurrence.

Other industries are self-regulated. Accountants self-regulate. Concerned that government might come along and regulate haphazardly, accountants presented their own regulation scheme through an industry group.

This allowed "the accounting industry" to stand before politicians and demonstrate what a good job they were doing at self-regulation so that politicians would not feel a need to intervene. This body representing "the accounting industry" surely does not represent all accountants, since so many disagree with moves in this direction. This method of regulation, while pleasant sounding, can be just as ineffective as government regulation. FASB, through a variety of decision-making methods, sets rules that stand between the accountant and the consumer. It is a small group of people getting together and stating what they believe is best, leaving the remainder of society without a say. This, in the end, leaves neither the entrepreneur nor the consumer fully in communication, and therefore not in full control of their relationship. Not allowing two people to be in control of their relationship limits the potential of the market. This method of regulation reduces innovation. This method of regulation tends to favor big players in a market, protecting them from upstart competition by increasing barriers to entry.

Some in the Bitcoin industry see these four methods of regulation and seek to move Bitcoin into the last method – self-regulation – which is unquestionably a horrible model of regulation for any industry, and an especially horrible method of regulation for Bitcoin, since it does the exact opposite of some of what makes Bitcoin so special: it increases the barriers of entry; it reduces potential for innovation; it puts in place gatekeepers; it centralizes authority; and it removes the ability of entrepreneurs to deal directly with the consumer in any of the variety of ways that the consumer and entrepreneur agree to.

Ask your accountant about FASB. Some accountants love it. They are trained to love it and to live life by its rules. The rules of the Bitcoin industry should be that there are no rules. As with so many other industries, the market will weed out some players and reward others. To be as innovative as an accountant, self-regulate. To be as innovative and responsive as a market can possibly be, let the market regulate.

Any compromise on this topic is a terrible one. "Yes, but if we don't self-regulate, they will regulate us," insist some. I've yet to hear a good explanation from the pro-regulation crowd as to how exactly government will successfully enforce regulation on an underground currency that operates across a dispersed network. Many difficulties might occur. Government can put in place barriers that can make life harder for those using the Bitcoin protocol, which would not be an attractive option.

It took significant resources to shut down a single website – The Silk Road – and the act of shutting down that single website appears to have had little consequence in the world. Government had special incentive to want to shut down Silk Road for the rampant illegal activity that took place on that site, a site that would allow users to only pay and be paid in Bitcoin. A month later, a Silk Road 2.0 was in place and many others were vying to take the coveted place of this heavily trafficked black-market website. Does the government have the resources to dedicate to shutting down two Silk Roads? Twenty Silk Roads? Two thousand Silk Roads? A guerilla force of freedom fighters is out there on the Internet with a strong desire to see frictionless online markets. If government backs down, they are called online free markets. If government pursues the users and operators, they are called online black markets.

No government has ever had the ability to eliminate the human desires that lead to the existence of a black market. Much more innocent and much more numerous are the people who simply want a frictionless online currency. Am I to believe for a moment that an FBI that took years to shut down the largest and most public black market for illegal narcotics on the Internet has the resources to force regulation upon the many thousands of people who want access to new types of financial instruments? That would be an example of overestimating the power of my opponents. Anyone who wants to restrain the power of the amazing revolution that is about to take place in the world's financial system is my opponent.

Be careful of anyone who seeks to regulate a technology that will throw the financial world on its head, making room for everyone at the table, with greater efficiency and consumer-oriented responsiveness.

Anyone acting to hamstring that process earns no respect from me and proves they deserve my disdain and distrust. No matter how slow you go, government will never catch up, so it's pointless to even try slowing down the tiniest bit. Doing so steals from the world the minutes, hours, days, years of joy that can be had by your amazing work. Press on. Press on with utter disregard for those who would slow you down.

Slowing Down The Innovators

Of course no one will walk up to an innovator and say, "Please slow down – you are moving too quickly." Doing so would entirely ruin the great value that an innovator can bring to society. It is best for an innovator to think years ahead of the rest of us. That is probably the greatest use for an innovator. Then why would anyone encourage an innovator to spend time on anything other than innovating? Ideally, an innovator in the Bitcoin space would spend as much time as possible innovating. Yet there is a movement among proponents of Bitcoin to call on government to regulate Bitcoin.

For some, the intention of seeking this regulation is to prevent even worse regulation from being foisted on the new technology by politicians and government officials who do not understand Bitcoin well. The inevitable consequence of this is that some of the most important innovators in the Bitcoin space will be further distracted from the work they are doing. Instead, they will have to pay attention to issues like how to properly fill out form BTC-XJ900 and comply with regulatory code 8 something 6.9(c)3 subchapter P0. Because I understand even a fraction of the potential of Bitcoin for the world, I am eager to see the innovators in the Bitcoin space develop the technology at a focused and fast pace.

Governmental Barriers To Entry

The Bitcoin space lacks testosterone. In that space, there are plenty of men, I mean chromosomally, and they probably mostly have radices, but they do not accept the risk-taking adventurous role that our society traditionally attributes to men. The woman nurtures and plays it safe; the man ventures out and takes risks. Society has long demanded that men step forward to bring change. There's some logic to those traditional gender roles in Western culture. There are drawbacks as well. Like a bunch of "women," the men in the Bitcoin space are largely twiddling their thumbs waiting for some other womanly man in some government office to give them permission to change society. If that's how it's all going to go down, we'll be waiting a good long time for permission.

Especially embarrassing is this idea of asking permission from some slimy, formless snail in a government office. Geez, what has become of American bravado that these are the permission-seeking Americans we have trying to innovate? Would the West have been won with that attitude? Pioneers came first, traders moved in, settlers after them, even more traders followed. Government showed up late in the game. I doubt government has ever been the first one into a promising societal trend. No need for Bitcoin entrepreneurs to suddenly change that truism of the world. Let government follow.

I could easily say right now, "It's all the government's fault" and, "If there were no governmental regulation, then Bitcoin would have already been big, would have already been changing the world." That would be a cop-out. What I really should be saying is, "If the people in the Bitcoin space were a little more gutsy, a little more ballsy (to use a truthful metaphor), then Bitcoin would already be big." Waiting for permission to change the world will bring no change. What's the worst they can do to you? Shutter your company so you have to start another one? More likely they will just end up deferring to you because you are the cock crowing the earliest and most mightily. Be a man. Stand up. Quit waiting for permission to change the world.

Technological Barriers To Entry

There are other barriers to entry for Bitcoin. You need some device connected to a network. Having a device connected to the Internet has been the norm worldwide for a number of years. Kenya, a third-world country, has M-Pesa, which allows currency to be transferred without a bank. All things considered, if an elderly Kenyan villager can pull it off, an American should be able to do the same, meaning that the technological barriers to entry aren't that high.

Bitcoin, however, remains an unreachable enigma for many in the US who would like some exposure to it. Many people active in Bitcoin make excuses such as, "There are too many governmental barriers" slowing down the ability for mainstream America to access Bitcoin. This tremendous potential is being capped up in a little bottle because, "We are waiting for regulators to issue a ruling" and it is being done just long enough for the big boys to get a foothold in the Bitcoin system.

Waiting is foolish. The technology to bring Bitcoin to regular Americans exists. The profit potential exists. So many people are just too damn scared to make it happen. This points to the key reason why people who develop technology lose control of the technology: among other reasons they tend to be more interested in the nuts and bolts of the technology than in seeing it succeed. Be bold. Ignore the regulators. Introduce your new Bitcoin technologies that will bring Bitcoin to the world.

The Barriers To Entry

The gatekeepers are still there; the walls have now come down. Big corporations, contrary to popular thought, use regulation as an added barrier to entry in their industry. Bank of America can take on the Federal Government and survive. They can kowtow and pay hefty fines and survive, chalking it up as the cost of doing business.

Upstarts, in order to succeed, must spend time not on innovating in that industry, but on compliance with regulation, which disproportionately challenges their resources. To be a successful bank you don't need to be the best for your customers; you need to be the best at handling regulators and be good enough to your customers to compete against the handful of other big banks who are also good at handling regulators.

This condition is the opposite of a free market and the big money changers love it. It limits competition and encourages the gobbling up of weaker but more innovative upstarts that are appealing to their customer base.

Finance is an example of an industry so heavily regulated that political entrepreneurs beat out market entrepreneurs with regularity.

Political Entrepreneurs And Market Entrepreneurs

Government can interfere in markets. It has the power to do so. In a free market, a brilliant interplay takes place between the entrepreneur and the consumer. Entrepreneurs compete fiercely for the consumer. Many entrepreneurs will not survive such contests and will be weeded out by the market. Those who step forward and rise to this challenge are market entrepreneurs. They seek to compete in a free market against all others at being the best at fulfilling the wants of the consumer.

Political entrepreneurs recognize that there is a shortcut that can be taken in this process. The shortcut distorts the market, reduces competition, makes it less likely that the consumer will be as pleased, slows innovation, and gives the political entrepreneur an advantage in the industry that otherwise might not have existed. Instead of appealing to the consumer in the marketplace, the political entrepreneur appeals to the politician. The politician intervenes in the marketplace in a way intended to minimize the feedback of the consumer and to give the political entrepreneur advantages over the competition.

Many forms of government intervention have the exact same effect – affecting the market in favor of the political entrepreneur who has structured his business model accordingly. A market entrepreneur tends to shy away from regulation. A political entrepreneur may actually welcome regulation.

The Worry Of
Government Regulation

The money changers will control a regulated Bitcoin. Those in the community who advocate for government regulation probably misunderstand the nature of government regulation and are exchanging long-term widespread benefits for short-term-focused gain. More sinisterly, they may exactly understand the nature of regulation.

Regulation tends to be favored in the market by big players or established players as a way to limit the potential of upstarts. Certainly, some in the Bitcoin space recognize this as the advocate for regulation. Upstarts introduce risk and destabilize an established market by innovating existing concepts and introducing new solutions. Upstarts increase the competition for consumers. Increasing regulation and adding other governmental barriers to entry makes it less likely that an upstart will successfully enter a market. Established corporations have protocol in place to handle regulation in a way that causes little disruption to the corporation. Upstarts tend to not have that luxury and seek to focus their resources on developing an improved product and reaching out directly to their consumers.

A relatively small number of people may talk the Bitcoin community into the need for government regulation. This really should not happen.

Regulation benefits today's Bitcoin "establishment." It will cement them in place for a lifetime. And is there really anyone deserving of the lifelong title "Bitcoin establishment" for a currency that didn't exist five years ago? It's a revolutionary, wild currency built upon an amazing security protocol and should remain as such.

Every revolution sees the revolutionaries taken from power, replaced with more stable figures. In doing so, the growth of the revolution is cemented into place and its gains are secured. In exchange, its future potential is lost. Instead of rushing to cement Bitcoin's gains into place like a Windows machine, let's leave it a little more Linux.

Regulators, politicians, and bureaucrats prefer the Windows machines over Linux for a variety of reasons, most of which are deservedly unappealing to the adventurous and innovative Bitcoin community.

Free Market

As ridiculous as it sounds, thirty-five years ago a telephone monopoly existed in the US. Free-market proponents were mocked when proposing that a government-enforced monopoly was wrong: "What will you have, three phone lines out the back of each phone and a button to choose which company you want to place the call with? Will you have three sets of phone lines and three sets of phone poles down each street?"

The only answer that could legitimately be given then and now is, "I don't know how, but when the free market is honored and the profit motive comes into play, I know that enterprises dealing directly with consumers will solve the problems that exist. In fact, such enterprises will probably even discover benefits we never knew were possible."

This is exactly what happened in telecommunications and other high-tech fields. It will happen in any industry exposed to free-market forces. Bitcoin will develop in ways currently unimaginable through these same market forces. The free-market proponents were proven right. They just needed government to back off a little for the entrepreneurs and consumers to work their magic.

The True Danger Government Poses To Bitcoin

During communist times in some countries, atheist governments supported churches financially. This initially seems contradictory. That is only because we have a skewed understanding of what help is. Aid from government tends to be damaging in the long run. What a government funds a government can control.

In those countries, the hierarchy of numerous churches became beholden to their atheist government. Furthermore, the mere act of taking the church, an entity that took its orders from something that was bigger than any state, and making that church suddenly beg to the state for money, knocked the church down a notch. It confused some of the message of the Bible by making the church officials bow to the state.

Long-term government aid causes dependency. Vibrant churches that could thrive when run by voluntary contributions from their members were now offered payments from the state. Parishioners slowly began to realize that their monetary contributions were not so important. After all, the state was paying the pastor's salary and for the upkeep of the building.

When you financially support an activity, you tend to feel more connected to that activity. You tend to take it a bit more seriously. You're invested in it financially after all. Government paying for a church has the net effect of weakening that church. It may feel like a favor initially, but government support is the exact opposite.

The last thing any advocate of an organization should want should be help from the government. Help from the government should certainly be the last thing any market entre-preneur wants. No matter how the aid is packaged, help from the government should always be denied. Government assistance also comes with a great deal of unintended conse-quences. Government should be treated suspiciously and kept at arm's length. No matter how much anyone in government intends to do good, the very mechanism of how government functions will cause the opposite to happen.

Government is incapable of touching the decentralized Bitcoin. Where we stand today, the only thing that will change that will be members of the Bitcoin community voluntarily accepting help from government. Any gov-ernmental involvement will slow innovation, reduce the contact between consumer and entrepreneur, reduce competition, and, depending on how close government gets in its attempt to help Bitcoin, may create more significant problems that would not be immediately apparent.

Government is generally incapable, at this stage, of harming the long-term success of the Bitcoin protocol and the many functions built on top of it. If one wants to look at it from the perspective of government or Bitcoin being in the lead, then it appears the Bitcoin community has the upper hand. By the very nature of Bitcoin, government is currently at arm's length, which is exactly where government should be kept.

Competition Is Good,
Even From Tired Old Companies

Competition is great for consumers and for innovation. Many entrepreneurs consider it to be a great thing because it pushes them to achieve their best, creating a far better version of their product than they would have any other way. Virtually every day someone sends me an article about how some established company or bank is looking into starting its own currency.

I welcome that. I also tire of reading such articles. They mean little. It's usually lacking in innovation – it's some variation of the dollar with some cool marketing slapped on it to fool the gullible. I'm excited to see consumers have an opportunity to flock to or avoid such products.

Experience shows, however, that many large, established companies are poor at innovating. They are used to a non-competitive market made that way by government regulation adding to the barriers of entry and deterring upstarts. Many companies have business models that show greater comfort for pushing investment toward lobbying rather than research and development.

It's laughable to imagine any technology from a company like that competing with Bitcoin, let alone supplanting it. Bitcoin offers so much that a centralized entity cannot currently match. It is the door into the future of never having to rely on another centralized entity asking for your trust. Marketing goes a long way, though, so who really knows.

Many industries produce products that are well-marketed, popular, and seen as total garbage by the industry aficionados. Also, I'm not omniscient. I, just like all other humans, am incapable of seeing the needs of every consumer. Otherwise, central planning would work. I look forward to seeing the market decide what the financial future will look like and what role Bitcoin and other cryptographic protocols play in that future.

Providing Access

Place yourself in the Bitcoin boom. The one selling the components will prosper – the hardware, the software, the services. They will interface between the confusing and complicated error-prone Bitcoin world and the rest of the world. You see, Bitcoin has no value to a consumer who can't use it. Most people can't use it. What can you do to make it accessible? Look out the window right now. The first person you see is the person you want to make Bitcoin accessible to. By providing that access, you add value for someone for whom it is valueless.

You probably don't recognize this, but if you are reading these words anytime in the five years after this is released, then you are probably an early adopter and well positioned to be a dominant force in some aspect of the cryptocurrency field.

How Entrepreneurs Are
Restricted From Healthcare

Venture capitalists for years have been scouring the US healthcare system trying to find investment opportunities. The terrain is poor. A key factor is that there is little opportunity for an entrepreneur to "touch" a consumer. Consumers are so well insulated by insurance companies and government that the market is incapable of functioning. Functioning would mean supply and demand, and price fluctuations, and ways for consumers to deal directly with providers through the most important mechanism in a market monetarily, which means they pay their own bills and make decisions with their own money.

As a result, there is simply no incentive for entrepreneurs to jump into such a saturated market seeking to innovate, reduce costs, or provide a higher level of service. This is truly a shame since there is so much potential benefit that can be had by letting eager entrepreneurs loose on the medical problems of our society.

America has quite the high-tech healthcare industry with a great deal of innovation taking place. The problem is that what is currently taking place would pale in comparison to a free market in healthcare where consumers could freely interact with entrepreneurs. Perhaps even more important than high-tech innovations are improvements in services that would take place simply because of this new dynamic interchange in the industry. Patients (consumers) would benefit from a healthcare industry more closely resembling other industries with high consumer satisfaction, low error rates, high levels of responsiveness, and transparent pricing.

Instead, we have dissatisfied patients, entirely clueless about the cost of care, being treated poorly, with little responsiveness to complaints, at significant risk from complications, sometimes lethal complications, from error-prone service. Many lives are saved, something for which we can be grateful to lots of good healthcare practitioners. It can be much better though. In virtually every industry both the upstart entrepreneurs and consumers would love the industry to meet the needs of the consumers even more effectively.

From a consumer's perspective, no other industry is as incapable of improvement in its current state as healthcare. The error rates and common accidental infections resulting from bad procedure kill many Americans each year. Hospitals are the third leading cause of death in the US, behind only heart disease and cancer. *The Journal of Patient Safety* estimates that between 210 thousand and 444 thousand deaths each year in the US are attributed to hospital errors. That's as much as one-sixth of all deaths that occur each year in the US – the equivalent of killing everyone in Atlanta this year, then moving on to Oakland the following year, and Miami the year after that.

Simply reducing regulation and changing the relationship between consumer and healthcare provider to one in which the consumer handles the money, just like in any other industry, would be enough to drastically improve the motivation of entrepreneurs to enter this space and solve challenging problems. Adding regulation will have the opposite effect, essentially chasing brilliant, eager entrepreneurs from the healthcare space.

Bitcoin, A Similar Concept

Bitcoin exists in limbo today. It is not free market, because it exists under tremendous threat of regulation or even illegalization, which influences the market. It's hard to feel comfortable making long-term plans in that environment, which is one reason why some in the Bitcoin space seek regulation – some government regulation is better than a sense of uncertainty for some people.

The reality is that life is constantly uncertain. Once you accept that Bitcoin will continue to exist whether or not it has government's blessing should be encouraging. A significant amount of the risk in the Bitcoin space has little to do with government. The Bitcoin space, as a startup environment involving a new technology, is inherently risky. That is part of what makes the space so exciting to work in, so dynamic and full of growth opportunity.

It isn't for everyone, which is why not everyone in history is remembered as a revolutionary who changed the world. Those who can court this risk and accept it as a vague and changing area of terrain that must simply be dealt with will be far ahead of those sitting on their hands waiting for who they evidently believe to be omnipotent and omniscient government to decide the financial fate of the future of the world.

Perhaps this will ruin the ending for you, but let's skip ahead nonetheless. When all is said and done, government can be counted on to make the entirely wrong decision about Bitcoin. Whatever that governmental decision is, it will, by definition, be wrong. That is the nature of government. That decision could chase some people from the Bitcoin space and will embolden others. Knowing now, far in advance, that government is going to be wrong, doesn't it feel good to know that you can simply shrug your shoulders at whatever government says, taking into account the reality that almost any decision from government, in addition to being wrong, will also come to be irrelevant.

The potential of the Bitcoin protocol reaches far beyond anything government has the ability to control. That's simply how the market functions. It's why plenty of black markets exist for anything government bans, and have always existed at any time throughout history. Add to that the decentralized technology, and we have this beautiful equation that renders the government seemingly less significant than ever.

There is nothing new to that. It's a self-fulfilling prophecy. If people want something badly enough, government has little ability to prevent those people from acting. If the people who see the potential of Bitcoin want it badly enough, there is nothing government can do.

This type of sentiment is clear back to the founding of the United States. The well-trained and technologically advanced British had a hard time containing the disorganized guerillas that opposed them. A guerilla force is difficult to oppose.

The US Government seeking to oppose a decentralized technology is akin to its going against a guerilla force of freedom fighters. These freedom fighters aren't necessarily ideological; they simply want government to step aside and let them deal in Bitcoin. They want freedom from that government intrusion in their lives. Not only is the government's fight against a decentralized group like that next to impossible; their battle against freedom fighters is immoral and will ultimately destroy the morale of any agency involved in it. It's a scummy fight on the part of the government. It's a scummy fight for a capable and decent individual to build his career around.

Bitcoin will be disruptive to the status quo. Government will seek to disrupt the disruption and maintain the status quo. Bitcoin and a series of other new technologies will prevail in disrupting the status quo.

Government will fall in line afterwards, ready to protect a new status quo, all the while pretending that it has a say, much like an impotent man with bravado.

Government Doesn't Understand Bitcoin And *The Wall Street Journal* Doesn't Take It Seriously

That's the best possible scenario. The heads of major exchanges could make Bitcoin standard overnight by introducing Bitcoin contracts there. But they won't. They don't understand it. Many of them can't talk about it for thirty seconds. That may seem like a foreign concept to you – that an intelligent, well-paid person doesn't understand something as rudimentary and potentially influential as Bitcoin; however, it is seldom understood in some circles.

It is spoken of jokingly and is generally dismissed. Some well-educated people can get stuck in a form of groupthink that makes them especially slow at catching on to new trends. Understandably, if you made

$100 million a year ignoring new trends as CEO of an established Fortune 500 company, you too would probably be excited to continue ignoring new trends.

Big banks can make Bitcoin their basis for payment systems. But they don't get it. They'd love to bottle it and sell it, but honestly, how can you sell an institutional client or a high-net-worth, annuity-loving individual on, "My payment system is built on 40,000 decentralized 'nodes' that I have zero control over."

This is a situation in which familiarity with the technology will probably allow customers to develop a comfort for the technology. Or, maybe there's no way for big institutions to be involved in something they can't control on their own or through government. It is outside of their current business model. To reach them as consumers, an entrepreneur will come along who can bridge that gap.

So many in the Bitcoin community are rushing to convert the world and rushing to convince. There's a problem with that, though: the sooner anyone happens upon Bitcoin, the less impressed they will be. The ideal is for the world to learn as slowly as possible about Bitcoin.

With every passing day, the Bitcoin space becomes increasingly ready for a grand unveiling, a grand presentation of what the space has to offer. It is a complicated system that requires one to suspend disbelief while listening to poor communicators speak of entirely unfamiliar topics. Every day, Bitcoin entrepreneurs wake up seeking to bridge that gap, seeking to make yet another system created by abnormally intelligent minds for sending ones and zeroes, into a system that intuitively makes sense to anyone who stumbles upon it.

Instead of forcing square pegs into round holes, you can stop rushing to convert the world, and let them recognize the value of Bitcoin more organically, so that the very first look they take at Bitcoin speaks to them on their level and makes as much intuitive sense to them at that time as it does to those who already understand Bitcoin today in its rough form.

On top of that, that discussion in which you try to rush people into Bitcoin takes so much time and so many resources. The better approach is to spend your energies developing new technologies, new entrepreneurial efforts, and to do so without fanfare. The rest of the world will catch up and will come to recognize what a treasure exists in the Bitcoin protocol.

Dedicate the next ten years to creating developments in the Bitcoin industry and you will be a billionaire. The marketers and cheerleaders are chattering, trying to buy your potential for pennies on the dollar to sell them to big banks and government for twice as many pennies on the dollar. They are nothing but paupers. Don't do it.

Recognize now what a wealth of knowledge you have when you act on it smartly. Google didn't go public until August 19, 2004. The company remained closely held even after going public. It's not because of a lack of value that Google didn't go public with so many competitors in the run-up to the Internet Bubble bursting. Nor is it because no one was interested. Everyone on Wall Street wanted to take them public. The owners simply wanted to maintain control of their company and to shape it into something special instead of making a quick buck.

Work on distinguishing yourself as an innovative entrepreneur in the Bitcoin space with simpler, clearer, easier, mightier, and faster answers to everyday problems, and the one or two fast-talking mindless marketers trying to buy you out today will one day be competing with the thousands of other fast-talking marketers just to get a cubicle on the same floor as your office. Ignore them. Keep doing the entrepreneurial work required to build the Bitcoin space. Few returns may come initially, then modest returns. Hang on and the world will catch up to you just as you finally feel ready to handle them.

Early on, Google didn't market. They waited. They knew they were going to be the biggest. They were going to dominate. They were going to influence the innovative terrain of the Internet beyond their dreams. With each passing day, they became so much more capable that they knew if they could get a customer to wait one more day they'd be even more amazing when that customer formed his first impression. Google wowed, only they didn't wow with the empty platitudes of sales pitches. Their mentality was the opposite of sales pitches – under-hype, over-deliver.

That is where the Bitcoin world can be: under-hype, over-deliver. So many want to see Bitcoin blow up, get huge overnight. What's the rush to see Bitcoin blow up?

It's usually ego driven. As if it were important to be able to say, "See – I told you." The people who want to see Bitcoin blow up today tend to demonstrate motives that are short term. I wonder if any single individual can say the right words to cause a currency to blow up.

It seems to be a societal phenomenon beyond the control of individuals; however, what an individual can do is build the best X in the Bitcoin space, the best Y built on the Bitcoin protocol, the best Z system of all cryptocurrencies. In doing so, value is added to the Bitcoin space that makes it possible to blow up. That's where an individual can affect Bitcoin – with ease, with affordability, with style – making the user experience of Bitcoin in some way better.

Time Is Of The Essence

Becoming a Bitcoin evangelist is futile work, likely with little reward. Trading the stuff is asinine unless you are an experienced trader. Investing in it is a fool's errand as it is so speculative. Making a niche for yourself in Bitcoin and being world class in that niche is how you will change the world.

You should want the world to catch on to Bitcoin slowly. And you should be working excitedly in a frenzy to develop the best you can before the world figures that out. At the cutting edge of society, where econom ics and technology intersect, money and talent are pouring into the Bitcoin space at a frenzied pace.

And you might be too late. You must act today or risk being just another one of those ponytail-wearing seniors who tell stories about how they were there. How they were in the valley when it all went down, how they were at MIT or Berkeley or somewhere else. They saw it all. And they missed it all. Their claim to fame (and it's only a claim) is having been there and watched things happen.

They knew A, they did acid once with B, they worked for C. Nope. That doesn't cut it. Amazing things are happening *today* and anyone in the know can be a player. You are in the know. The world is awash with easy money. You can be a player. Investors are looking for returns and can be generous in funding startups. The Bitcoin environment is full of problems that need solving. The market is so virgin, not only do consumers not know that the problems exist; they don't even know

Bitcoin exists. You can be a player. An innovator. You can change the world.

The easy-money policy is garbage and opposition to it is often linked as a source of Bitcoin's genesis and its rise. Accept the easy money as a temporary reality you aren't likely to change. By becoming an entrepreneur in the Bitcoin space, you become a recipient of that easy money.

That offers tremendous potential for overinvestment in Bitcoin R&D, right now. Right now, this moment, your startup can be hot. It's not the amount of money a market would normally allocate to something as potentially unpredictable as a Bitcoin startup, but the easy money needs an outlet. That overinvestment is bad when looking at the market as a whole. It is good for the individual who realizes it is a bubble leading to overinvestment that will not handle a down market well. Recognize that you are receiving a temporary subsidy from the rest of the economy.

You, today, are the outlet; a bubble will form in the Bitcoin industry. Plan for that – plan for the easy money to dry up and if you're ready for that you'll be both entrepreneur with developed products and services, and a competitor in the industry ready to buy the talent, technology, and assets of companies that didn't plan. You see, Bitcoin research, development, and entrepreneurship will grow. It just has the chance to grow even more quickly right now than it has had in the past or will have in the future.

The popping of the Internet bubble did not stop the Internet from developing; it merely chased away some of the flashy people who weren't so serious. After the Bitcoin bubble pops, the space around the Bitcoin protocol will keep growing – irrespective of what the coin is doing. It will be the technology that is so important and will lead to market growth dominated by those who were financially ready for that stage in history.

Only an asshole can't make money in the situation you stand in right now. Even some assholes will do it. Do it now: stake out a piece of "land" and begin cultivating it. Stay focused on your land, make it grow green and expand.

Most people can't do that. You're different. You get Bitcoin. You get how it works. If you need to improve, you can do so in under an hour. You know some of its pros and cons. You really can put this book down right now and start developing a product that solves a problem in the Bitcoin space.

You are about to be even more amazing than you already are and the world will soon know it. Or not. The choice is yours.

You can be a sad cliche if you want. Old age, a beat-up car, a ponytail, kitschy Hawaiian prints and smelly open-toed sandals can all be your future if you choose – where you can tell the stories about how you used to know the guy who now owns his own island. The island is a justly deserved reward for changing the world; the ponytail is a justly deserved reward for not doing so.

You can be a player, all because you were a little quicker in figuring out a new technology and worked at improving it.

Conclusion

Bitcoin is a crap currency and a bad investment in a world of terrific investments built on a protocol that will come to change the world. Look at those facts honestly, apply yourself in that space with vision and focus, with dedication and vigor, with a technician's mind and a pollster's ear and you will be a Bitcoin billionaire, perched in a place even more prestigious than those who rode the last world-changing wave – the Internet wave – that we are today building on.

Your name, a household name, your riches generational, your reputation – that of one who changed the world.

By chance, by fate, by grace, or by some other force, you have been placed in the position you are in today. Will you take on that role that is being offered to you? Anyone can be a speculator. Anyone can cheerlead. Only a few will have the gall to step forward and proclaim to the universe that they will carve a place in history for themselves as a person who will always be looked back on and called great.

ABOUT THE AUTHOR

Allan Stevo is a founding member of the New York Bitcoin Center where he served as the head market maker during its early open outcry operations. In that capacity Stevo has appeared in some 200 international, national, and local media  sources, among them CNN's Inside Man with Morgan Spurlock, Bloomberg, Reuters, Huffington Post, and The Wall Street Journal's Market Watch.

Stevo organized the Schiff-Tucker Bitcoin debate between the two Austrian school brains, has been a founding member of several Bitcoin trade organizations, was an early organizer of the first Bitcoin Super PAC, and has organized fundraising events for Bitcoin friendly politicians.

He is the editor of 52 Weeks in Slovakia and contributor to The Daily Caller, The Hill, Economic Policy Journal, and Mises.org.

In Spring 2012, Stevo became a best-selling author with a book covering the nuts and bolts of winning a grass-roots political campaign. He lives and works in New York City.

www.ingramcontent.com/pod-product-compliance
Lightning Source LLC
Chambersburg PA
CBHW021405170526
45164CB00002B/511